PROJECT BOLD LIFE:

THE PROVEN FORMULA FOR TAKING ON CHALLENGES AND ACHIEVING HAPPINESS AND SUCCESS

Edward M. Kopko

BOLD
BUSINESS
2020

Advance Praise for Project Bold Life and Author Ed Kopko:

"Ed Kopko's book **Project Bold Life** is beyond motivational; it's transformative. Faith is a precursor to boldness, and often times people have faith, but lack the boldness to go beyond self-imposed limitations. **Project Bold Life** gives ample examples of people that have shattered any notions of limits, on their potential towards pushing past any obstacles in their way. Living a Bold Life annihilates doubt, and frees the spirit towards greatness. I'm Living a Bold Life. Come join me." - *Bruce George, Founder of the Genius is Common Movement, Co-Founder of Def Poetry Jam on HBO*

"There are very few self-help books that are page turners. Ed Kopko's Project Bold Life is one of them. The insights keep coming like lightning flashes in a thunderstorm on steroids. It is not only a guide to success it is a guide to life. Read this book, it will improve your life. It has improved mine." - *Anthony Stimac, President, Musical Theatre Works International, Author of Upcoming Book, "The Journey"*

"As a parent and a professional, managing work-life challenges can sometimes be daunting. Ed's book gives thoughtful advice on how to successfully manage work-life challenges and live a life of no regrets. Every parent should read this book! And then tell their children to read it as well!" - *Dr. Marion Brody, Radiologist and Parent*

"Ed has a gift for making things simple, with wonderful stories, and actionable steps to enable you to lead a bold life." – *Neddy Perez, Chief Diversity Officer, McCormick & Company*

"Bold is a gift, a weapon and a lesson. If you don't learn the lesson, you won't be able to use the weapon against adversity and bring the gift back to your organization, your community and to benefit your own development. Ed Kopko offers us access to the timeless importance of being Bold...learn, fight, give: the numbers don't lie!" - *Bruce Craven, Author of "Win or Die: Leadership Secrets from Game of Thrones", Professor at Columbia University*

"Ed's message of achievable bold goal setting should resonate with every talent-based organization. Anyone interested in advancing within their career, or any company interested in fostering a culture of pipeline development and internal mobility, will find these principles to be vital. Every talent management office should encourage their team to read this book - Project Bold Life inspires enthusiasm and action regardless of where you sit within your company." - *James E. Taylor, Ph.D., Chief Diversity, Inclusion, and Talent Management Officer, UPMC*

"This book has many deeply insightful and practical ways of creating and acting upon transformational life goals. Freeing oneself from the fear of stretching to achieve bold life goals is a gift this book delivers." – *Michael J Critelli, CEO MoveFlux Corporation, Retired Chairman and CEO, Pitney Bowes*

"Ed has worked extensively to bring diversity and inclusion to the global business arena, imparting a message of hope and positivity for all. This book is an extension of that message, and it outlines the path individuals can take to attain fulfilling, bold lives!" - *Pamela McElvane, Publisher of Diversity MBA Magazine*

"Crave personal and professional success? Desire to live a life without regret? There is no better way to achieve it than embracing the system Ed Kopko so thoroughly provides in Project Bold Life. I wish I had Ed's goal-setting tools, advice and stories when I was launching my career. This book is solid gold." *–William A. Lederer, Chairman and CEO, iSOCRATES LLC, Adjunct Professor, Graduate Media Management Program at The New School*

"I recommend **Project Bold Life** by Ed Kopko as an ideal addition to those freshman college courses designed to introduce students to college life and a consideration of life's purpose. At the university, I would urge parents to encourage their students to study that for which they have a passion because this is a sure way to success. By success I meant the optimal balance of talent, time, and treasure – the talents we develop and deploy for the betterment of self and society; the use of time so that the personal and professional dimensions of life are in balance; and the treasure we start with, accumulate, and give away, recognizing that luck plays a part and we should always say, 'Thank you.' *Project Bold Life* is a terrific guide to help students become the author of their own lives instead of merely an actor in someone else's script. Buttressed by scientific research as well as personal stories, **Project Bold Life** does all this and more." - *Dr. Robert A. Scott, President Emeritus and University Professor Emeritus, Adelphi University*

This book is dedicated to my family

Past, Present and Future

Acknowledgments

Writing this book has been a heady effort. It has made me a better person and has taught me much. The old adage that the best way to learn a topic is to teach is amplified when writing a book. I have learned a great deal attempting to put this topic to paper. I hope you will find the content valuable and apply some of the concepts.

The genesis of this book has been within me for years. How to live a full happy life with no regrets is something that I have wrestled with since I was young. Many people I have encountered have wrestled with similar thoughts. The fantastic people that I have interviewed and worked with throughout my career helped me develop and reinforce the framework of ideas that have guided me during this journey.

This book is about you, not me. It is not a memoir or lessons from Ed. It is a conglomeration of learning from the many people I have been lucky to know. I hope you will see me as the scribe and developer of the framework and lessons.

There are many great people to acknowledge for their important roles in this book. It was a multiyear effort. All the research, interviews, graphics, websites, databases and illustrations involved many talented people.

First off, Jim Genia worked with me closely on this manuscript as editor and researcher and deserves the first and biggest shout out. We worked endless hours on all elements of the book and he was a constant smart source for me to bounce ideas and help make my ideas come to life. More importantly, he was a positive force, particularly when I would hit the inevitable blocks.

Dawna Stone, an accomplished author and businesswoman, deserves the next shout out for inspiring me to write this book and being a confidant, advisor, intellectual contributor and coach.

Brittany Birsner played a key role in the formation of the book and its messaging. She helped develop my thinking regarding the importance of speaking to youth and using more elements to do so. She was the "go-to" for first ideas on all types of elements and messages. Her keen eye helped me improve the messaging.

The additional team behind this book was vast and amazing.

I would like to acknowledge the programming team that built the Bold Life Assessment, which became an important foundation for the book. This includes Joy Clarin, Cherry Arimado, Michael Robles, Marlon Aromin, Dwight Navarro, Eustaquio "King" Manzano, and Lorelie Perez. They developed a custom program that enabled us to gather information on how people viewed their lives and goals. It was almost a year-long effort and the survey and reports people received were amazing. Dawna and Ellen Madden deserve major kudos for developing the questions and designing the report that participants receive.

I would also like to acknowledge the video team from Bold Business that assisted me in creating great content and helping develop the stories of some of the interviewees for the publication. The footage became an important part of the research for the stories. This includes Doug Rifenburg, Will Linthicum, Lou-Jico Jarlego, Anj Perez, Viktor Toledo, Gaius Merza, Jeremy Feria, and Camille Holgado.

The illustrations and creation of Boldy was a huge effort. Brittany, Dawna and Ellen helped in his initial concept.

A major shout out to the talented Cris Hipolito, an amazing creative illustrator. Also, kudos to Enrico Alonzo and Rosli Ali.

My author website had many great contributors. Thanks go to Brittany, Manuel "Wacks" Siocon, Ron Rivero, Christine Sese, Cristina DeLima, and Joan Kadibhai.

Photography for the site and back cover were taken by the talented Cecilia Lagerman of Lagerman Studio LLC.

I would also like to thank my sons, Michael and Matthew, who were early readers. The framework for the book was shared with them from an early age and I parented them through the principles. I learned some important lessons as a result!

Of course, my mom, Martha Kopko, is the best mom and cheerleader a son could ever have.

Finally, I would like to acknowledge my wife, Lenore, who encouraged me to share a little more about some of my personal side. She also put up with me isolating myself to write and create. She particularly influenced me to more fully develop my thinking and writing about challenges and setbacks. Chapters 2 and 3 are better because of her.

Contents

SECTION I: LIVING A BOLD LIFE

Introduction 1

Chapter 1 – What Does it Mean to Live a Bold Life? 13

Chapter 2 – Taking on Challenges 22

Chapter 3 – The Blank Sheet(s) of Paper 38

Chapter 4 – The Bold Life Formula 45

Chapter 5 – The Bold Life Pillars 56

Chapter 6 – The Cycle of Life and Your Bold Life Goals
.... 65

Chapter 7 – Defining Bold Goals 81

Chapter 8 - Creating Meaningful Change 97

Chapter 9 – Creating Your Bold Life Action Plan 112

Chapter 10 – Choosing to Act, Choosing to Succeed
....138

SECTION II: LIVING BOLD: FINDING YOUR PASSION, GOALS AND SUCCESS

Chapter 11 – The Most Rewarding Pillar: Health 150

Chapter 12 – The Most Challenging Pillar: Achievement
.... 159

Chapter 13 – The Most Coveted Pillar: Career 169

Chapter 14 – The Most Confusing Pillar: Finances 184

Chapter 15 – The Most Sought After Pillar: Relationships
.... 190

Chapter 16 – The Most Overlooked Pillar: Giving Back
.... 204

Chapter 17 – The Most Enlightening Pillar: Experiences
....216

SECTION III: ARE YOU READY TO LIVE A BOLD LIFE?

Chapter 18 – The Bold Life Assessment: Crunching the
Numbers..222

Chapter 19 – Believe and Achieve 228

APPENDIX I: THE WORKSHEETS.................................232

APPENDIX II: INDEX...248

Section 1: Living a Bold Life

Introduction

"The greatest danger for most of us is not that our aim is too high and we miss it, but that it is too low and we reach it." - Michelangelo Buonarroti

I started writing this book before the COVID-19 pandemic struck, and entered the home stretch with the world under lockdown. The underlying message was always one of boldness—during the course of my life, I have met numerous people who have done great, inspiring things, and I wanted to both share their bold accomplishments and explain how they did it all. Despite the lockdowns, the unrest and the economic chaos, that message remains unchanged.

Why? Because being bold is still possible. In fact, it's actually more important.

Boldness is what separates the average from awe-inspiring. I want to be more of the latter than the former. We only get one life to live, so why not seize all the opportunity and glory the world has to offer? Should COVID-19 change that?

In picking up this book, chances are the notion of creating a Bold Life for yourself is a lot more appealing than having a life where average and ordinary is the status quo. That's great! I want to thank you for seeking out boldness!

How is a Bold Life achieved? A big component of the equation is goals.

Having goals is important, and at some point, everyone sets goals for themselves. When we are children we learn about goals.

From waking up earlier to get ready before the bus comes to take you to school, to studying a little bit harder for a better grade on a test, to going the extra mile to earn a spot on the starting lineup of the varsity basketball team, we learn early on that setting goals is a key ingredient in the "secret sauce" that makes success taste so delicious.

Most kids have Bold Goals. They want to be athletes, famous actresses, doctors, teachers, social media influencers and more. It is this naturally unchecked optimistic spirit that is so wondrous in children. Kids have beautiful dreams for their future.

As adults, that penchant for setting goals continues. Yet for some, those big, inspiring dreams can sometimes be put on the shelf. In a recent study conducted by Zety, only 33% of people achieve their childhood dream job.[1]There are important practical to-do's that must be done, and the big dreams can be put aside. Yet some of the important stuff is actually important stuff.

Getting into a good college and earning a degree? That's a noble cause that entails a lot of self-improvement, and it requires goal setting.

Securing a job and career that both fulfills us and pays the bills? This is another fantastic thing to strive for, and it requires more goal setting.

Starting a family and raising kids? Lots of goals are required to make this one work, especially if you want your spouse and kids to be happy.

Realizing your dreams of becoming a doctor, karate black belt, CEO, or marathon runner? Overcoming a disability or illness or learning to walk again? These are all clearly examples of bold lives, and as such, need more than just ordinary goals.

---

[1] Survey conducted by One Poll for Zety with a sample of 2000 Americans from Nov 8, 2019- Nov 11, 2019. https://www.swnsdigital.com/2019/12/these-are-the-most-popular-jobs-kids-dream-of-doing-when-they-grow-up/?fbclid=IwAR0b84Ut3X9nHy2QpYAjxGaqtS3Lqg-1sfgotfXWOKx-IkOa9D38VNIqI5c

They need Bold Goals!

MOST PEOPLE KNOW A BOLD GOAL WHEN THEY HEAR IT.

In fact, anything truly worth accomplishing--anything that points toward a life lived boldly--requires more than just deciding to set your alarm clock an hour earlier, spending an extra 30 minutes going over your notes from class or staying after basketball practice and shooting a hundred extra baskets. It requires things like inspiration, an Action Plan, and perseverance.

Remember when I said that having goals is important? Well, it is, but for the true success and happiness that comes with living a Bold Life, it's those Bold Goals--and especially the sense of accomplishment from realizing them--that make it all worthwhile.

The notion of a Bold Goal isn't a new one. Whenever someone told you to "reach for the stars" or "aim high," they were really telling you to set Bold Goals so you could create your very own Bold Life.

This is not your typical motivational book (although I do hope to give you some motivation!). Instead, it is intended to help you set and accomplish the Bold Goals that will enable you to build the big Bold Life you choose to live. Let's emphasize the important part of that sentence: the Bold Life **you choose to live.**

Everyone's Bold Life is deeply personal, and as a result, this is not a one-size-fits-all method. After all, yours is not a one-size-fits-all life! You've got your very own set of aspirations and desires, and—perhaps more importantly—you've got your very own set of setbacks and challenges you have faced.

The choppy waters created by setbacks and challenges are a part of life, but that doesn't mean they're easy to navigate. You've probably faced tough times and loss, so you know this. I know I've faced tough times and loss—I woke up one morning to find that my beloved 46-year-old wife had unexpectedly passed away. But from this tragedy, I learned that only by getting past these setbacks and challenges can we truly achieve great, bold things.

Throughout the chapters, I have included over a dozen real-life success stories to help you see how a Bold Life is possible for everyone, regardless of social or economic challenges.

The stories come from people of all walks of life, people who have created Bold Lives regardless of their circumstances. I hope these stories help you realize that you can have a Bold Life -- a Bold Life you can be proud of and that inspires. It is up to you to live it. No one can live your Bold Life for you, and no one owes a Bold life to you. It is yours and yours alone to make.

There are many reasons to set and work to achieve your Bold Life. Research shows that people who have big dreams are happier, more motivated, rebound from setbacks better and live more purposeful lives.

- Bold Goals give you the energy to get going in the morning and keep at it later in the day.
- Bold Goals provide hope and inspiration to act, even in the face of adversity and challenges.
- Bold Goals are even an essential leadership tool. They serve to inspire others.
- Finally, Bold Goals help provide focus and direction in your life.

For those of you who need more convincing that seeking a Bold Life offers many benefits, I have created the "33 Reasons to Live Bold" list for you.

33 REASONS TO LIVE BOLD

1. Living boldly makes you happier

2. You will wake up in the morning with enthusiasm to achieve

3. You will be inspired to go the extra mile

4. You will be resilient when facing adversity

5. You only have one life to live, so why not?

6. Fortune favors the bold

7. Mediocrity is not fun!

8. You will inspire others

9. A Bold Life requires Bold Goals, and people with Bold Goals have more energy for life!

10. People are drawn to those who are striving to reach their Bold Goals or have accomplished them - the world comes to you because of your goals

11. Bold living crushes drudgery

12. Problems find solutions

13. Is there a better choice?

14. Bold Goals help develop new strengths

15. Bold Goals drive you to be all you can be

16. You will manage your time more efficiently

17. Your life will have a sense of purpose

18. Accomplishing Bold Goals teaches you to deal with obstacles easier and with less stress

19. You will feel better about yourself

20. Studies show that if you have a rich, productive life--a Bold Life--you tend to live longer and healthier

21. Bold lives set the best examples for our kids

22. A Bold Life is something to be proud of

23. A Bold Life gives you a stronger sense of satisfaction over what you've accomplished

24. People who live Bold Lives tend to have fewer regrets

25. A Bold Life is a courageous life

26. People who live Bold Lives stare fear in the eye... and make it run!

27. People with Bold Lives make more friends

28. A Bold Life with Bold Goals achieved makes you feel accomplished and content

29. Attaining Bold Goals teaches you to give it your all

30. Striving for a Bold Life lets you create your future

31. Striving for a Bold Life lets you learn from the past

32. "Even God lends a hand to honest boldness."
   - Menander, Ancient Greek playwright

33. Living a Bold Life is a great life!

$PBL = PI + S/G + AP$

Project Bold Life is divided into three sections encompassing several chapters to help you not only appreciate the process of realizing a Bold Life but also apply it to your unique situation and goals. But **what will truly help jumpstart the process that puts you on your path are the worksheets**, which makes up the resource material in Chapter 16 and is also available for download at EdKopko.com/PBLWorksheets.

What tools are contained within these worksheets?

- You will find a worksheet called the Pillar Ranker that will help you determine which aspects of your life are most important to you
- A Pillar Planner to enable you to iron out a time frame on when you want to accomplish your goals
- A worksheet called the Goal Refiner will help refine your meaningful goals until they're nice and bold
- A Bold Life Formula worksheet that lays out your Action Plan, which you will sign and give to someone who will hold you accountable and encourage you to stay on track
- And many more!

This book is also based upon compelling science[2] that increases the chances of making

---

[2] In particular, I point the reader to "Changeology: 5 Steps to Realizing Your Goals and Resolutions" by John C. Norcross as a great

successful bold changes. Research over the last 30 years has dramatically increased our knowledge of change, and some systems of change now have long histories of scientific study. The methods we apply here were developed from these studies.

These studies have helped tens of thousands of research participants live happier and healthier lives. The Formula is built upon these proven methods and science.

The worksheets are designed to help you easily follow the proven steps. The Formula and worksheets will help make your Bold Goal journey sharper and more defined. Together, they will increase your chances of success. We apply these principles to a dimension of change that is not typically the first one considered. Most people think about changing a negative dimension. We are focusing on positive dimensions - the appealing and inspiring idea of change. In particular, not how to fix a bad life but how to live a Bold Life.

In addition to the worksheets, **the book will go into greater detail about the *Project Bold Life* Seven Pillars and break down the various aspects of life into discernible areas.** Inspiration for a Bold Life always comes from the Pillars. Choosing a path can be challenging for many and the Pillars are an important framework.

Within each of these chapters, I will cover the specific yet simple steps to living that aspect of your life to its fullest, and at the same time, provide you the opportunity to be inspired and motivated in determining which Bold Goals are right for you.

starting point. In Chapter 2, I will share more about the science when describing the formula.

Throughout the chapters, I have added over a dozen real-life success stories to help you see how a Bold Life is possible for everyone, regardless of social or economic challenges. In tandem with each story, many have completed worksheets to illustrate how that particular person took a requisite step in finding their own brand of success within the Seven Pillars.

Ultimately, the stories—and the completed worksheets accompanying them—will show how the Bold Life Formula was applied to each person's unique circumstances and enable you to visualize how those formula components can be applied to your life.

The stories are meant to inspire, and they include:

- Justin and Kaisorn McCurry, a couple who decided that they wanted to retire in their thirties, and stuck to a plan that made it happen.
- Pam Sloate, a woman born with a debilitating disease and through perseverance was able to freely walk again and inspire others. She is "The Little Engine that Tried."
- Scott Young, a man who managed to complete an MIT undergraduate education in just a year… for free.
- RJ Garbowicz, an entrepreneur whose laser-like focus and determination to succeed has brought his Bold Goal within reach.
- Marilyn Reyes Scales, an ex-convict who, after her incarceration, wanted her family back—and took the steps needed to accomplish that.
- Titus O'Neil, a troubled youth who took stock of his life, made the commitment to turn himself

around, and eventually became a pro wrestling superstar.

- Dr. Laraine Lloyd, a grandmother who got her doctorate degree just before her 70th birthday.
- Vinod, a man who wanted to better himself, and with a new job, altered the course of his family's arc for generations to come.
- Henry Stifel, a quadriplegic who's spent much of his life striving to help those confined to wheelchairs walk again.
- Father Robert Sirico, a Catholic priest who worked to educate the clergy on the notion that helping others doesn't preclude personal success.

This book is built upon the thousands of interviews and interactions I have had with many successful people from all walks of life, including CEOs, company founders, political leaders, teachers, athletes, actors, and the unsung who have accomplished amazing personal and professional Bold Goals. It is from these people that the Bold Life Formula was born. Most importantly, their stories help provide real-life examples that a Bold Life can be had by anyone!

Since the summer of 2019, over 1,800 people have participated in the Bold Life Assessment online, which consists of 49 questions that develop a detailed look at how people are practicing living bold through the Seven Pillars. Many of the statistics and findings from the assessment are included throughout the book.

But perhaps more importantly, the data collected from the Assessment participants has shown us that a shockingly high percentage of people need help with goal setting – 84% in fact!

Seeing that so many respondents were unable to clearly articulate a specific goal showed me that there was most certainly a need for the lessons contained within *Project Bold Life* – and it shaped much of this book's content and message.

You can also take the assessment for yourself at www.boldlifescore.com. It's fun and free and will provide you with an in-depth analysis of how boldly you're living your life and share tips for moving toward the life you desire.

Complementing the worksheets, research and stories are cartoons featuring "Boldy," who—like you—wants to live a Bold Life. You can follow along with his journey and share in his experiences.

If you're reading this book, then building a Bold Life is important to you. No matter where you are, or how far you may be from your desired life, *Project Bold Life* here to help you on your journey. With your personal commitment and the guidance provided throughout this book, your Bold Life is attainable.

Thanks for opening this book. I hope you will find it to be a long-term friend in your journey to living a fabulous Bold Life. To live bold is to live to your full potential. Let's start your journey today!

Say "hello" to Boldy! He's going to be taking this Bold Life journey with you!

Chapter 1 – What Does it Mean to Live a Bold Life?

"Whatever you can do, or dream you can, begin it. Boldness has genius, power and magic in it." - Johann Wolfgang von Goethe

"Boldness" is a word that has many connotations.

Boldness implies courage and bravery, and it suggests an ability to put aside your fears. Boldness is also associated with advancing good and justice while shining a spotlight on less admirable pursuits. Similarly, boldness is linked to strength, power, and assertiveness. The more confident we are in our actions, the bolder we are said to be. Taken as a whole, each of these definitions and attributes helps us better appreciate what boldness truly represents.

But when we describe boldness in our lives, its meaning may not be quite as clear.

What is a bold life?

Is a bold life simply living well, or is it something more?

Pursuing boldness in our lives demands seeking a higher level of excellence. A Bold Life (*note the capital letters*) is one where you strive to realize your fullest potential to become the best person you can possibly be. A Bold Life is one that gives your life meaning and purpose, and at the same time, provides immense joy, happiness, and a sense of fulfillment. It reflects a life where your actions and behaviors not only enhance your own life but offer a positive impact on the lives of others.

As you can see, a Bold Life embraces a broad perspective that can involve every action you take in every aspect of your life.

At the same time, a Bold Life also involves your values and your beliefs. Those who pursue a Bold Life choose to live their life according to inherent character values, and they boldly stand up for their beliefs. Living your best possible life also requires that you respect diversity and the uniqueness of all individuals while honoring community and all of humanity. And it involves being generous, kind, compassionate, and caring.

Through self-reflection and a deeper understanding of personal values, those seeking a Bold Life find congruence between their beliefs, their character, and their pursuits.

Understanding this, it might seem that aspiring to and achieving a Bold Life might only apply to those with the greatest skills, talents, and resources. But this couldn't be farther from the truth!

Living boldly is something any of us can choose regardless of our position or status. Embracing the pursuit of a Bold Life can occur at any age and at any time. And while the definition of a Bold

Life may vary from person to person, it's available to each of us.

We only have one life to live, and all of us enjoy the opportunity to make it the boldest life possible.

Naturally, each person's definition of a Bold Life will vary since each of us are unique.

However, by analyzing countless self-help books, talking to numerous experts, and asking everyday people what it means to live a Bold Life, priceless insights have been gained. These insights have identified seven key areas that serve as sources of inspiration in defining what a Bold Life means to each of us.

These key areas, or Pillars, are ***Health, Achievement, Career, Finances, Relationships, Giving Back and Experiences.*** Collectively, these are the Seven Pillars, and they are the foundation upon which a Bold Life is made.

Ultimately, a Bold Life is one where you unapologetically strive to realize your dreams through a commitment to excellence in specific areas of your life. From this perspective, living your best life can focus on a single facet of your life, or it can involve several of the Seven Pillars. Through the Seven Pillars, you can identify specific aspects of your life where you would like to live more boldly.

You might choose to focus on a single Pillar, or instead, you may define new goals in several.

Regardless, each Pillar reflects an area where boldness can be pursued based on your current perspective and life situation.

The Seven Pillars encompass many important aspects of life where bold pursuits might be identified. Not only can Bold Life pursuits involve your life's achievements and career successes, but they can also involve relationships and meaningful experiences.

A Bold Life may also include health and wellness goals and aspirations.

And a Bold Life tends to embrace a broader view of community, society, and the world in which we live. By adopting these perspectives, you will be better able to identify your most important priorities - and that can help you realize your greatest potential.

The pursuit of a Bold Life can best be achieved through three key steps:

(1) Identify your meaningful, inspirational goals from the Seven Pillars

(2) Stretch yourself to specify your own version of boldness

(3) Create an Action Plan to make these goals a reality

Each of these steps is essential in helping you realize your life's potential. These steps have been incorporated into the Bold Life Formula, and they will be addressed in greater detail in the chapter that follows to aid you in your pursuit of living the boldest life possible.

As part of the final section of the book, the Project Bold Life Worksheets will be provided to help you further contemplate specific actions to take in realizing a Bold Life.

From ranking which Pillars are more important to you, to refining your Bold Goals, to laying down a concrete Action Plan, the Worksheets are the tools that will help you get on that horse and gallop away from a regular life toward your Bold Life (and if you fall off that horse, the Worksheets will help you get back on it!).

Beyond the Worksheets, you will be encouraged to complete the Bold Life Assessment, which is fun, free, and takes as little as 10 minutes to complete. This Assessment offers additional insights regarding your Bold Life journey that can assist you in determining the best strategy for success.

Unlike many other assessment tools, the Bold Life Assessment does not simply provide a single, cumulative score. Instead, you will receive an overall score as well as individual scores for each of the Seven Pillars. This breakdown of scores will provide you with information that better identifies areas where additional effort is needed - and tell you where you are already exceptional. The Assessment scores will even provide comparisons to others who are the same age and gender.

The journey in pursuing a truly Bold Life is a lifelong process. But like most experiences, the journey offers greater value than actually achieving the goal. As you move through each of the steps of the Bold Life Formula and consider each of the Seven Pillars, you will gain a deeper appreciation of yourself and the goals most important to you.

And with the instruments and insights offered in this book, you will enjoy an opportunity to truly create your boldest life possible. Choose to live boldly, and you will soon enjoy all the wonderful benefits these pursuits provide.

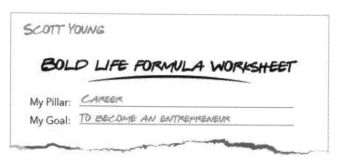

SCOTT YOUNG

BOLD LIFE FORMULA WORKSHEET

My Pillar: CAREER

My Goal: TO BECOME AN ENTREPRENEUR

In 2011, Scott Young was a 26-year-old college graduate when he made his decision to pursue his Bold Goal and change his life forever.

After graduating from the University of Manitoba with a bachelor's degree in commerce, "a middle-ranked Canadian school I could afford," Scott found that his degree did not prepare him properly for what he really wanted to do. His goal was to be an entrepreneur – he wanted to run his own business. He found his commerce degree had prepared him to be a "grey suit" in the corporate world. Scott had no interest in becoming a "grey suit". Something needed to change. He needed different skills to become an entrepreneur.

Scott has shared his thinking about his next steps in his fascinating book, "Ultralearning: Master Hard Skills, Outsmart the Competition and

*Accelerate Your Career." He did not know it, but
in his journey to success, he would soon be
applying the Bold Life Formula.*

*Scott decided he needed to go back to school and
learn computer science, where he could learn
how to design products, websites, algorithms and
more. These were skills Scott determined were
important to become an entrepreneur. He needed
to learn how to build and create something. The
problem was he was not excited about another
four years in school and more college debt. A
four-year computer science program would have
a huge opportunity cost for him, both in time and
money. He was not prepared to pursue his dream
if that was the price he would have to pay. His
Bold Life would be stalled by his unwillingness to
pay the price.*

Fortunately, there was a different way.

*While researching schools to pursue his
education, Scott "stumbled across a class taught
at MIT and posted online." Scott had discovered
the world of MOOCs, Massive Open Online
Courses! Better yet, the courses were free with all
test materials provided, and Scott could take the
courses at his own pace whenever he wanted.*

*MOOCs today have come a long way since the
time Scott discovered his first class. Much more
work was required back then to figure out what
could be accomplished online. Now it is quite
easy.*

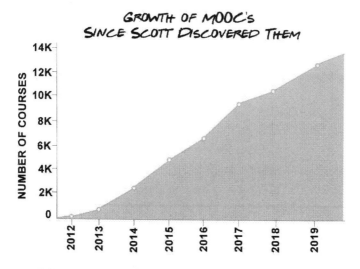

GROWTH OF MOOC's
SINCE SCOTT DISCOVERED THEM

By the Numbers: MOOCs in 2019
Statistics do not include China

As of 2019, 110 million students have taken classes offered by over 900 universities. More degrees and certificates are available from different universities compared to back when Scott started. More stats on MOOCs are available from www.classcentral.com.

In his book, Scott describes the process he followed. He was excited about the one course he had found. He asked, "If anyone could learn the content of an MIT class for free, would it be possible to learn the content of an entire degree?"[3]

---

[3] "Ultralearning: Master Hard Skills, Outsmart the Competition and Accelerate Your Career". Scott H. Young, Harper Business, Harper Collins Publishers 2019

After six months of research, Scott dubbed his project the "MIT Challenge" and decided he would and could take this project on...

Chapter 2 – Taking on Challenges

"Don't be afraid to take challenges in life as without taking challenges you'll be unable to see what's your real capability." - Anurag Prakash Ray

Before getting into the formula and worksheets in future chapters, we need to talk about challenges. Challenges can be the reason you never try to live a bold life or they can stop you in your journey. **Dealing with challenges is a "must-have" skill set.**

In a chaotic world, challenges are pervasive. Some of these challenges can be extremely foreboding. They can stop you from being able to focus and work on anything. Loss of job, financial ruin, health issues, and struggles to provide for yourself and family can lead to enormous stress. During these points in time--which can be important turning points in many cases--thinking about living a bold life is the furthest thing on people's minds. Survival becomes the mantra, and thinking about a big future is pushed aside.

I am not going to sugar coat these issues and tell you to just move on. It is more complicated than that. In fact, how you deal with your challenges is an important element in recovery and moving forward. **Everyone suffers and faces setbacks. They are part of the human equation.** So much so, actually, that we can learn from others the steps to follow to make progress and find hope and inspiration in their stories.

In future chapters, you will read the inspiring stories of people who overcame setbacks or difficult conditions and accomplished great things. After all, it is comforting to know that we are not alone in dealing with issues, and we can find role models of people who successfully took on challenges. Now, however, we'll focus on some perspective.

In a TEDx talk on September 25, 2019, Dr. Lucy Hone opened her speech by asking the crowd some questions.

"1. If you ever lost someone you truly love, ever had your heart broken, or struggled through an acrimonious divorce or being the victim of infidelity, please stand up or raise your hand.

2. If you have ever lived through a natural disaster, being bullied, or made redundant, please stand up.

3. If you have ever had a miscarriage, if you ever have had an abortion or struggled through infertility, please stand up.

4. Finally, if you or anyone you love had to cope with mental illness, dementia, some form of physical impairment or cope with suicide, please stand up."

Virtually everyone in the crowd that day was standing or had their hand up. **Her point: everyone suffers setbacks and challenges.**

I have created a listing of setbacks and challenges people face below. I am sure you will find a few that have come into your life. When you review this, ask yourself these questions: "If I am not the only person to deal with setbacks, what lessons can I learn from others? How might I improve the way I deal with them? Will I be a person to let setbacks define me and hold me back?"

Everybody has them!

Dr. Hone's point is that challenges and setbacks are common, so common that it's possible to objectively compare the problems that stand in your way with the problems that others have had to deal with to get where they are.

And don't forget that some challenges are positive, meaning that they stand in the way of something very rewarding. Once these positive challenges are overcome, you—in one way or another— come out better for having overcome them.

Here's another word cloud, this one laying out some positive challenges:

TYPES OF POSITIVE CHALLENGES

Everybody has them!

The lyrics to Kelly Clarkson's hit song "Stronger (What Doesn't Kill You)" addresses the issue of setbacks from a slightly different angle, but in the same vein.

> "What doesn't kill you makes you stronger
>
> Stand a little taller
>
> Doesn't mean I'm lonely when I'm alone
>
> What doesn't kill you makes a fighter
>
> Footsteps even lighter
>
> Doesn't mean I'm over 'cause you're gone"

In her Ted Talk, Dr. Hone advises, "Don't lose what you have to what you have lost." While Clarkson's song has hurt and anger as part of the motivation to get stronger, there are many instances where smart approaches to dealing with setbacks and loss are required.[4]

For another perspective, consider Viktor Frankl, a famed psychologist and Holocaust survivor. In his book "Man's Search for Meaning", he said: "...everything can be taken from a man but one thing: the last of the human freedoms—to choose one's attitude in any given set of circumstances, to choose one's own way."

In other words, when it comes to life's curveballs, it ultimately doesn't matter what happens to us. Instead, **what matters most is how we respond to those things that happen to us**.

This chapter will lay out three steps that Dr. Hone defined that day in beating those feelings of despair and hopelessness, steps that encompass elements of the Seven Pillars, the Bold Life Formula, and even the inspirational stories that make up the backbone of this book. But the first thing you must understand when tackling these seemingly insurmountable challenges brought about by our feelings is that...

It's All in Your Mind

When I say, "It's all in your mind," I don't mean the challenge or setback you are experiencing is not real. The big ones that shake our confidence and stop us in our tracks are typically very real. How you chose to address these challenges is up to you. You must make a choice. You can let the setback win or you can choose another path. Henry Ford famously said, "Failure is the opportunity to begin again, in a more intelligent manner."

---

[4] For more about Dr. Lucy Hone's approach, I encourage you to check out her book, *Resilient Grieving: How To Find Your Way Through Devastating Loss*

[5] You control your approach to setbacks with your mind. Henry believed it meant to start again.

Randy Scott, the author of the book "Zenpowerment" and founder of Zenpowerment.com website, puts the onus directly on you for the thoughts that are coloring your outlook. In the chapter, "The Power of Choice and Meaning", he writes, "Choice is something we DO, not something we HAVE."[6] He further encourages people to act and not wait for motivation to occur. He writes, "Motivation does not create action. **Action creates motivation.** When we choose decisions of action, it is in the action that creates the motivation. When we act, dopamine is released in the brain, which helps provide motivation. If you ever don't feel 'motivated" to do something, just start, and the motivation will come."[7]

All of these things point to one immutable fact: **Most people don't realize that we can choose which thoughts to entertain.** Whichever thought comes up, we tend to attach to them like some precious treasure, whether they are empowering or disempowering. When we realize that we can let go of thoughts that do not serve us, we become free of their power.

So let's get to those three steps, shall we?

The Three Steps to Overcoming

The setbacks that stand before you may seem daunting. Insurmountable, even. But it's vital to know that

---

[5] For more on Henry Ford and his leadership philosophy read Bold Business's piece https://www.boldbusiness.com/human-achievement/bold-leader-spotlight-henry-ford-captain-of-industry/
[6] Scott, Randall H., *Zenpowerment, Your Path to Peace, Power and Purpose* (1998), pg. 53
[7] Ibid. 77

you can live with setbacks and still go on to achieve a Bold Life. In fact, most--if not everyone--who have accomplished something inspiring did so in the face of adversity. Despite the challenges in their way, they achieved something great.

They were successful, and you can be, too. You just have to remember the three steps to overcoming the setbacks and obstacles before you.

The trick to taking on challenges--and fighting through the despair that can so often come when obstacles stand in the way of our goals and dreams-- can be distilled down into three simple steps. They are:

- **Acceptance**
- **Find Some Positive**
- **Move Forward**

This may seem like an oversimplified cure for something that can often feel complex and overwhelming, but don't forget that after a century of medical innovation, the best treatment of the common cold is still chicken soup - simple cures work!

So consider these steps when setbacks are getting in the way of your pursuit of a Bold Life.

Step #1: Acceptance

Denial may be one of the biggest impediments to progress, but the antidote is always acceptance-- acceptance of the nature of your circumstances, and acceptance that you've lost something or there is something in your way.

It is very common for people to face challenges but fail to recognize that they are actually facing one. Their biggest obstacle is suddenly not that which stands before them, but their failure to see that they have something in their way.

The truth is, there is no shame in admitting that something stands in the way of your ability to accomplish or achieve something. It doesn't matter if the obstacle is grief, regret or fear, or if the obstacle stems from poor finances, ill health or unfulfilling career. Denial of the existence of the problem is the true first obstacle to overcome.

Of course, after accepting that something is impeding your progress or keeping you from achieving your goals, acceptance of the nature of the obstacle is important, too.

Later in the book, we'll go into greater detail some methods for setting and realizing goals. But for the purposes of this discussion on how best to overcome challenges, the most salient point is the crucial first step of acceptance.

Step # 2: Find Some Positive

The second step in overcoming setbacks is to find some positive. When finding positive, there's a particular tenet that is vital to remember: Not all challenges are negative.

Sure, a cancer diagnosis is a pretty negative thing, as are dire financial straits or a loss of a relationship that meant a lot to you. But many challenges have positive aspects--and some are almost 100% positive. If you were to visualize a spectrum, with setbacks on the very negative end, over on the positive side would be challenges that actually have a lot of upside to them. For example, the Bold Goal of meditating for 500 consecutive days is objectively a challenge--a person would have to make time to achieve such a feat, and they'd have to hold firm to their commitment to get those 500 days done. Those are most definitely challenges. But they're not negative ones.

A difficult workout session is a challenge, but the health benefits that come with completing that workout certainly don't make it a negative one.

Even some of the setbacks and challenges that can clearly be labeled as negative can have a positive side to them. The aforementioned cancer diagnosis, while a grave medical condition, can lead to a very healthy change in dietary habits, or improved family relationships, or even just an appreciative outlook on life.

I previously mentioned Henry Stifel. He suffered an injury as a teen that left him paralyzed, but that setback—a very major one—never stopped him from realizing his Bold Goal of helping others. In fact, his condition gave him both the perspective and drive needed to succeed.

Ultimately, there can be a positive aspect to almost anything. The trick--especially when it relates to taking on challenges--is to find that positive, clutch it close to your chest, and use it as a glimmer of hope as you move forward.

Another way to find some positive within the challenge is to understand that the challenge, and the act of overcoming it, is what makes people bold and great. That challenge is, therefore, a necessary component of the equation.

No one ever became a huge success without facing challenges. No one ever became an accomplished athlete without facing challenges. No one ever became anything easily - the challenges were an integral part of it all, and it is those challenges that helped them rise above.

If climbing mountains weren't challenging, would they even be considered an impressive feat?

Later on in this book, we'll delve into the comparison between relative goals and objective goals, and how goals that are a stretch yield far greater rewards. But for the purposes of the discussion in this chapter, just understand that **you WANT the challenges that lie in the path of achieving that stretched out goal**. Those challenges are what make that Bold Goal so very worth it! Courage and perseverance are ingredients to accomplishing great things.

Another concept I find meaningful is related to stress. Most people think of stress as a negative but it isn't. Similar to positive and negative challenges, stress can be the same. My favorite reminder? From great stress comes diamonds. The most perfect stones in the world come from stress. Do you want to be a diamond? If so, then learn to embrace the stress that inevitably comes with it. Again, it's your choice.

Step #3: Move Forward

Putting one foot in front of the other, both literally and figuratively, may seem like an oversimplified solution to what can be a complicated problem, but it truly is that simple. Whatever you are feeling--be it discouragement, depression or despair--is, ultimately, a transient feeling.

As the **Austrian poet Ranier Maria Rilke said, "Just keep going. No feeling is final."**

In Chapter 11, you will read the story of Pam Sloate, a very accomplished woman who has had to manage through not one but two huge medical challenges in her life. Yet despite them, she keeps moving on. She refers to[8] herself as "The Little Engine that Tried." On her blog, she writes:

> You see, The Little Engine That Could started out as The Little Engine That Tried. "I think I can" goes to the heart of the trier. Although we don't always beat the odds, we persevere in the face of them. Triers may not ascend the victory stand but always earn the "E" for effort. We never disdain second place or honorable mention, instead focusing on whom to thank for getting us there. Indeed, triers remember to enjoy the scenery along the way in case we miss our intended destination. Triers needn't worry about leaving a trail of regrets lying in the dust.

One of the famous quotes from the "Little Engine That Could" book is "I think I can, I think I can." The difference between success and failure can be that simple thought. Try. For me, I have long been influenced by a similar but older quote:

"FOR THEY CONQUER, WHO BELIEVE THEY CAN."

— VIRGIL

    None of the setbacks you face have to define your life, and the quicker you can move on and get on the path towards your goals, the better off you are.

---

[8] I highly encourage the reader to check out Pam's Blog. https://dystoniamuse.com/2013/05/27/the-little-engine-that-tried/

This is, of course, usually easier said than done, which is why you must have the right mindset and inspiration.

Later in this book, we'll dive much, much deeper into the process of determining true inspiration and refining them into Bold Goals (and an Action Plan). But for now, let's just focus on how inspiration relates to moving forward when you're mired in setbacks and challenges.

Where does your true inspiration lie? Is it contained somewhere in the goals you've set for yourself, or is it elsewhere? **Sometimes, putting the "I" in inspiration is the difference between making a goal that has real meaning to you and making a goal that doesn't.** That "I" signifies that "I really want this" - a mantra that, when repeated, means you're more likely to succeed at what you set out to accomplish. And it requires knowing why.

Knowing why you want to do something is the great differentiator, the secret sauce for success, and once you know why, the answers to any subsequent questions of "how?" and "what?" become more easily solvable.

How does one determine where their true inspiration comes from? The first step is figuring out from which of the Seven Pillars--Health, Relationships, Career, Finances, Achievement, Experiences and Giving Back--the inspiration stems from.

This can be a tricky prospect, so let's consider the story of a mother.

The mother wants to be able to pay for her child's college tuition in a few years. But to do so, the mother needs a career that will afford her that financial ability. If the mother were asked to pinpoint where in the Pillars her inspiration lies, at first glance, it might seem like the

Pillar of Career or the Pillar of Finances might be the answer. Even the Pillar of Giving Back might seem like it applies. After all, she needs something of all of them to achieve her Bold Goal, right?

RELATIONSHIPS

The answer is actually Relationships because what drives her is the love she has for her child, a love that inspires and motivates her into doing whatever is necessary to provide that college education for her daughter. Whatever she does in regards to Career and Finances is just a stepping stone to what she really cares about, an action step in her plan to make her Bold Goal a reality. Her "ultimate why" is her relationship with her daughter, and understanding and acknowledging that ultimate why means that if the mother were to fall off the horse at any time (like if she were to lose her job), she'd recognize her true inspiration and motivation, and get back on the horse!

By knowing that her true inspiration lies in the relationship between her and her daughter, the mother has a clearer understanding of her "why" - and that understanding is just the thing that will help her put one foot in front of the other and move beyond the setbacks and challenges that arise.

On a personal note, I've gone through these three steps after facing significant setbacks and losses in my life. I will go into greater detail about that in the next chapter, but let me tell you now: they work.

So you're facing setbacks and challenges, and you've been given some perspective on how to view these challenges as not necessarily that difficult compared to what others have faced. You've also been shown that challenges are often an important component in achieving greatness. Finally, the three steps to overcoming have been laid out--acceptance, find some positive and move forward--and you've been given the recipe for the secret sauce of inspiration. What now?

Now it's time to figure out if you need to get back on your horse after falling off or start anew with a blank sheet of paper.

Chapter 3 – The Blank Sheet(s) of Paper

"Nothing in this world is worth having or worth doing unless it means effort, pain, difficulty. No kind of life is worth leading if it is always an easy life. I know that your life is hard; I know that your work is hard.... I have never in my life envied a human being who led an easy life; I have envied a great many people who led difficult lives and led them well."- Theodore Roosevelt

On August 26, 2004, my life was tragically changed forever.

I awoke around 6 am like I usually did and walked into my master bathroom. I will never forget what I saw that morning. In front of me was my wife, slumped over the sink. She was in her night robe. I immediately pulled her into my arms to try to see what was wrong. It took me only a few seconds to realize the gravity of the situation.

We had a wall phone in the bathroom, and I dialed 911 as fast as I could. I cried out for help from my two teenage sons, who were asleep. They came running, and I asked them to help direct the medics into the house. Within minutes, emergency professionals had arrived, but it was too late.

I held her until help came into the bathroom. During those few minutes, I could feel the cold of her body and her lack of responsiveness. Her expressionless face told me what I did not want to hear. My wife was gone. The young, healthy and fit woman I married and loved had unexpectedly left me. The grief and despair that I dealt with over the coming hours, days, weeks, and years are impossible to describe. It changed me forever.

At some point in everyone's life, there comes a moment of despair. It can spring from the grief that follows the loss of a loved one, it can grow out of disappointment--like from failing to accomplish a goal--or it can come from feelings of hopelessness. This moment (or moments, because there certainly can be more than once in a lifetime) is inevitable, a natural part of the human condition.

Everyone deals with this despair in their own way. Some let those feelings overtake them, putting their dreams and desires on the backburner as they hunker down in their mental bunker and simply try to survive.

Others turn those crippling thoughts into fuel for the fires of motivation. Though they may grapple with the same despair and hopelessness, they opt to use those negative feelings to spur them on. I want to re-emphasize the need to choose.

In the previous chapter, I wrote, "How you chose to address these challenges is up to you. You must make a choice. You can let the setback win or you can choose another path."

When my wife passed, I had a choice to make.

Obviously, anyone adhering to the notion of a "Bold Life" would choose the positive path. When faced with losing a loved one, mourn, but turn that sadness into things that honor and celebrate the memory of the person gone. (Ultimately, I knew that my wife would not have wanted me to live a sad, unfinished life.)

When faced with the sudden, unplanned loss of a job, they take that moment of uncertainty to refocus their career goals and hone their direction. When faced with a natural disaster, economic downturn, or global shutdown, they seek out the silver lining, the opportunity hidden within the dark cloud, and make the most of a rough situation. In essence, the person living a Bold Life overcomes those challenges--whether they're within themselves or without--and comes out on the other side a better person.

The question, then, is not whether you should move forward towards your goals, but how best to achieve them or redefine them.

Should you dust yourself off, get back on the horse and resume galloping towards your goals?

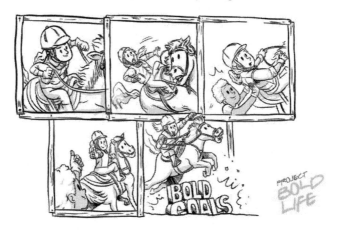

Or should you take this particular setback or challenge as an opportunity to reassess and recalibrate? There's no shame in the latter--no shame whatsoever in seizing the blank sheet of paper that is the future and drawing your masterpiece upon it.

Whether you're getting back on the horse or making a brand new plan to achieve your goals, the Bold Life Worksheets that I will walk you through later on will be a big help.

Maybe you're at a point where a setback has you rethinking your life.

Maybe you've hit a bump in the road and you're looking for some help getting back on track, or you're happily plodding along but want to juice it up some.

Regardless of the circumstances, I have good news for you. Going through the Worksheets to understand all the components that go into setting Bold Inspiring Goals that give you meaning, creating a realistic Action Plan, and applying the Bold Life Formula to get where you want to go applies. They are designed to help you succeed!

Knowing How to Choose

You're faced with a setback. You've accepted the nature of the challenge, you've found something positive to focus on, and you're moving forward. But you're wondering if you should continue on towards pursuing your goal, or if you should embrace the blank sheet of paper and start over with new goals and new plans on how to reach them. How do you choose?

Losing my wife was a definite challenge, but I also looked for positive, as Dr. Hone suggests. It brought my family closer together--which grief can sometimes do. I did not view my wife's passing as something that forced me to say I had to start over again. I was inspired by the substantial work in front of me within the other Pillars of my life. I had accomplished a lot in them already but was not finished.

I was a father to two great sons, sons who still loved and needed me, and I loved and needed them. I was involved with charitable organizations and making impacts. I was CEO of a company with 6,000 employees who relied upon me for leadership and direction. These accomplishments and responsibilities helped convince me that I didn't need to start over with a blank sheet of paper. Instead, I needed to get back on the horse and resume my journey. I had lost my wife, but I did not lose my entire life.

The blank sheet of paper wasn't what I needed, but again, some may need to start from scratch, and that's perfectly fine.

Some may think they need the blank sheet of paper, yet an assessment of the other positive things going on in their lives would indicate that they might be better off just redesigning their Action Plan in the Pillar(s) impacted to accommodate their new situation.

For example, the sudden loss of a job might not necessitate a dramatic change, especially if your Relationships Pillar contains a family or network of friends that can give you the love and support to help you keep moving forward.

Of course, a certain degree of change might be needed. Since my house was where my wife and I had made our lives together, and everyone in town would constantly ask me how I was doing, I felt like I needed a change to facilitate my recovery during the mourning phase. It was emotional for me to be asked how I was doing every day. Or walk into the same bathroom. So during the next year, I moved away from the town I loved—a dramatic change, for sure, and yet a necessary one. In the grand scheme of things, it didn't require a wholesale reassessment and retooling of my goals and the plans I'd made to reach them.

Ultimately, only you can gauge whether or not you need to start over fresh with the blank sheet of paper or keep going forward. Just keep in mind that the Worksheets (and the Bold Life Formula) are your tools to determine your true goals, refine and stretch them into Bold Goals, and figure out the right Action Plan to get where you want to be. It doesn't matter what you choose, but the Worksheets will help you succeed!

Remember that analogy I used in the previous chapter about the greater the challenge, the greater the reward? It's also true for preparation--the greater the preparation, the greater the reward. And the Worksheets, when done correctly, are the preparation for that greater reward. They will help you climb that big mountain!

Chapter 4 – The Bold Life Formula

"Let the steps I take toward my destiny be bold ones – for I know I am bold enough to walk this path." - *Anonymous*

When we speak of a Bold Life, words such as fearlessness, confidence, ambition, adventurousness, and strength may come to mind. But two important aspects of boldness may not necessarily be appreciated when we begin to contemplate the term.

These two aspects are encapsulated by the words "novelty" and "perseverance". Both reveal a great deal about how to pursue a Bold Life, and as we will discuss, they also help explain how the Bold Life Formula can help guide you in realizing your boldest life possible.

What is the Bold Life Formula? The Bold Life Formula represents the three essential steps required to facilitate your pursuits of realizing a Bold Life.

The steps are sequential in nature, meaning they should be performed in order. Because if they are, they will build upon one another and help better ensure your success in attaining results that define what a Bold Life means to you.

To put it another way, each step provides the foundation for the subsequent step, and by completing all three, tangible changes will occur that will lead you toward your goals.

But while the Bold Life Formula is pretty specific, the values ascribed therein are personalized and specific to your own values, beliefs, situation, and desires.

Naturally, each of us has unique circumstances and preferences. We enjoy different dreams and define boldness in ways that give each of our own lives meaning.

While the Bold Life Formula does provide a basic algorithm that anyone could use to define their Bold Life pursuits, it also permits a personalized approach. This aspect of the Bold Life Formula acknowledges that the definition of a Bold Life for one person is not necessarily the same for the next.

With this in mind, the figure below represents the Bold Life Formula. Although it looks fancy, it is very simple to understand.

$$PBL = Pi + S^2G + Ap$$

A Bold Life equals one or more Pillars plus a stretch and specific Goal plus an Action Plan. Breaking down the Formula...

PBL means Project Bold Life, i.e., the quest you undertake to make sure you are living your boldest, most fulfilling life possible.

Pi means a Pillar that inspires. It helps you classify the inspiration that drives you towards your Bold Goal.

S²G means a specific and stretch goal, meaning your goal must be specific (and not too broad), and it must not be too easily attained.

AP stands for Action Plan, which is the detailed plan that contains the steps and milestones needed to accomplish your Bold Goal.

The Bold Life Formula is designed to help you attain true boldness by creating the necessary foundations from which it may be pursued. From a generalized perspective, the Bold Life Formula provides an algorithm that guides you from goal setting to a plan of action. Yet, at the same time, it also allows the goals and actions you pursue to align with your specific abilities, preferences, and life situation.

The first step of the Bold Life Formula requires you to identify meaningful goals that define your Bold Life. As mentioned above, your inspiration for these meaningful goals comes from the Seven Pillars, which will be discussed in much greater detail later in the book. But for now, we will just say that each of the Seven Pillars can serve as an area where you might consider an array of Bold Life goals.

I previously mentioned Titus O'Neil (real name: Thaddeus Bullard). His meaningful goal involved rising above the trappings of a disadvantaged youth to become something inspirational. Actress Vivica Fox had a meaningful goal centered around career success. Father Robert Sirico wanted to help others. Can you see where in the Pillars these goals would fit?

At different stages of your life, different Pillars will likely be more relevant to you. For example, you may have an emphasis on career when you're younger, or health when you're older. However, each always represents a source of potential inspiration when it comes to identifying specific Bold Life goals.

In addition, for those who have more than one source of inspiration, choosing a Pillar (or Pillars) might be problematic. After all, if you value both health and career, which should you focus on first? What if your inspiration lies in three Pillars? Or four?

If the paths to each Pillar begins with a door, then choosing which door to walk through can sometimes cause paralysis – a paralysis of choice!

WHICH DOOR WILL YOU CHOOSE?

The second step of the Bold Life Formula then requires you to "stretch" yourself in defining the boldest nature of your meaningful goals. If a truly Bold Life is to be pursued, then this requires taking yourself to the edge while testing your limits.

These may involve relative goals that compare you to others or to a particular benchmark - like running a marathon and crossing the finish line in record time.

Or they may simply be personal goals that invite value and deep meaning to your specific life situation and circumstance - like learning to walk again after a debilitating injury.

Having defined which goals are most meaningful to you, this second step of the Bold Life Formula specifies the boldest nature of these goals relative to your own life.

Lastly, the final step of the Bold Life Formula requires an Action Plan so that your Bold Life goals can be effectively attained. Having invested thoughtful reflections into what inspires you and what provides deep meaning to your life, you must now transform these thoughts into actions.

Remember the "door to the Pillars" analogy? A good Action Plan will help you pass through the right door and travel on the path towards your goal.

The right Action Plan helps ensure that your aspirations for a Bold Life materialize and that Bold Goals are attained. After establishing the essential foundations in the first two steps of the Bold Life Formula, we will then invest energy into creating a personalized plan of action to foster your ultimate success in attaining a truly Bold Life.

If you're confused about which Pillar or Pillars to choose, or which door to walk through, there's a Worksheet meant to help you: the Pillar Ranker.

PILLAR RANKER

	IMPORTANCE	TIMING	WHY
HEALTH	○ Very Important ○ Important ○ Not Important	○ Now ○ Later ○ Much Later	_____ _____ _____
FINANCES	○ Very Important ○ Important ○ Not Important	○ Now ○ Later ○ Much Later	_____ _____ _____
CAREER	○ Very Important ○ Important ○ Not Important	○ Now ○ Later ○ Much Later	_____ _____ _____
ACHIEVEMENTS	○ Very Important ○ Important ○ Not Important	○ Now ○ Later ○ Much Later	_____ _____ _____
RELATIONSHIPS	○ Very Important ○ Important ○ Not Important	○ Now ○ Later ○ Much Later	_____ _____ _____
GIVING BACK	○ Very Important ○ Important ○ Not Important	○ Now ○ Later ○ Much Later	_____ _____ _____
EXPERIENCES	○ Very Important ○ Important ○ Not Important	○ Now ○ Later ○ Much Later	_____ _____ _____

- HEALTH — Both physical and mental well-being
- FINANCES — The fiscal wherewithal to survive and thrive
- CAREER — Work that fulfills
- ACHIEVEMENTS — Accomplishments you are proud of
- RELATIONSHIPS — Family, friends and everything in between
- GIVING BACK — Charity and volunteering;
- EXPERIENCES — Those memorable things that make life worth living

IMPORTANCE
VI - Very Important   I - Important

TIMING
Now   Later   Much Later

PBL = (PI) + S+G + Ap

PROJECT BOLD LIFE

Which areas of life are most important to you? The Pillar Ranker can pin down when you want to tackle any Bold Goals within those particular areas. For example, some may see goals pertaining to health as most pressing now, and while they want to have a career that makes them feel fulfilled, maybe they want to wait a year or two before pursuing it. Or maybe they want to set goals in multiple Pillars.

Remember: People who prepare properly are properly prepared to succeed – and achieve their Bold Goals! These Project Bold Life Worksheets will help you prepare.

The pursuit of a Bold Life is also a strong level of dedication and commitment to realizing these goals and implementing your Action Plan. Without perseverance, boldness cannot happen. Therefore, in order for you to get the most out of the Bold Life Formula, you must persevere in your efforts to be the boldest you can be!

As you navigate through the book, you will spend the most time defining your own meaningful goals and bold pursuits. Best practices regarding effective goal setting will be discussed in subsequent chapters to help you in this regard.

Both an overview of the Seven Pillars will be provided and detailed discussions involving each Pillar will come separately. By the time you reach the final chapter, you will have ample guidance to help you best define your own personal Bold Goals.

Once those goals are set, you will then be ready to construct an Action Plan that will serve as your unique roadmap to the Bold Life you desire.

JUSTIN AND KAISORN MCCURRY

BOLD LIFE FORMULA WORKSHEET

My Pillar: FINANCES
My Goal: TO RETIRE AT 33

FIRE is a growing movement that gained momentum with Millennials but has since been taken up by Gen-Z'ers and more. It stands for Financial Independence, Retire Early. It is a movement predicated on the concept of setting a Bold Financial Goal! It has now gotten a following that is inspiring more and more people. Justin McCurry is a great real-world example of living the FIRE approach.

Justin, a husband and father of three, retired in 2013 at the age of 33, after never earning more than $69,000 per year in his job. His wife, Kaisorn, retired in 2016. Her top earning year was $79,000, her last before retiring. Together they now enjoy financial freedom in a way many people just dream of. How did they do it? They followed the Bold Life Formula. They had an inspiring committed goal from the Bold Life Pillars

(Pi), plus a stretch specific goal (S²) and an Action Plan (Ap). PBL=Pi+S²+Ap works!

Justin lives in Raleigh, North Carolina, and now occasionally posts on his blog, www.rootofgood.com. (I encourage you to read his blog as it is filled with lots of great info.) He updates his family's financial status monthly for the world to see.

At the end of June 2020, the McCurry family's vital financial stats were:

*·	Net worth for the month increased $41,000 to $2,063,000*

*·	Income for the month of June was $6,244 and expenses were $2,311.[9]*

*·	Justin has been retired for seven years and his net worth continues to grow, and he continues to spend less than he earns.*

The important aspect of the Formula to highlight here is the plan that Justin and his wife set for themselves – an Action Plan that had strategic initiatives for the big picture, and more detailed steps to take for the day-to-day, month-to-month, and year-to-year.

And the numbers don't lie!

---

[9] https://rootofgood.com/june-2020-financial-update

ROOT OF GOOD'S EARNINGS & WEALTH

	My Salary	Mrs. RoG Salary	Additions to Portfolio	Portfolio Total
2004	48,000	0	15,000	64,000
2005	49,000	5,000	101,000	183,000
2006	55,000	40,000	75,000	295,000
2007	56,500	49,000	66,000	371,000
2008	64,000	45,000	73,000	304,000
2009	60,000	46,000	71,000	478,000
2010	64,000	56,000	68,000	662,000
2011	68,000	63,000	85,000	697,000
2012	69,000	62,000	102,000	940,000
2013	69,000	69,000	80,000	1,244,000

	Post Retirement Income	Portfolio Total
2014	12,000	1,351,000
2015	56,748	1,503,000
2016	38,467	1,680,000
2017	39,366	2,037,000
2018	43,133	1,871,000
2019	48,942	2,261,000

The McCurry family followed the three key FIRE components. The website www.playingwithfire.co defines the FIRE formula very clearly:

> Smart, often middle-income earners are using a simple formula of high savings rates (50-70% of their incomes) + frugal living (minimalism) + low-cost stock index

fund investing (Warren Buffett's standard investment advice) in order to reach financial independence within short, usually around 10-year periods of time.[10]

This quote captures the essence of the Bold Life Formula! A Bold Life equals an inspiring goal (financial independence) + Specific and Stretch (enough income to retire in 10 years) + a plan (high savings, frugal living and smart investing). All the ingredients were in place.

---

[10] https://playingwithfire.co/whatisfire/

Chapter 5 – The Bold Life Pillars

"Be bold enough to use your voice, brave enough to listen to your heart, and strong enough to live the life you have always imagined." – Unknown

In defining a Bold Life, its precise meaning naturally varies from person to person. We are each unique with special interests, talents, and abilities. Therefore, it is understandable that what one person defines as a Bold Life may not be the same for another.

However, many common areas of focus are shared among everyone who boldly seeks to be the best they can be. These common areas are what we have defined as the Seven Pillars. By gaining a deeper appreciation and understanding of their relationship to a Bold Life, you will be better able to define the specific Bold Goals you desire. In fact, your inspirations for a bolder life all start within the Seven Pillars!

The Seven Pillars were not simply chosen at random. Numerous experts and professionals - as well as surveys of broader populations - have provided insights in this regard. In compiling all of this information together, seven key areas became readily apparent.

No matter what your situation, every Bold Goal exists within one of the Pillars. Therefore, by delving deeper into each one, the opportunity for inspiration in pursuing a bolder life can be revealed.

Recall that the Seven Pillars are the following:

- *Health*
- *Achievement*
- *Career*

- *Finances*
- *Relationships*
- *Giving Back*
- *Experiences*

When considering these Pillars individually, some common features and some differences are bound to exist among individuals.

For example, a Bold Life pertaining to the health Pillar for one person might focus on a physical goal (like getting a black belt in karate) while another may assign greater value to mental or spiritual wellness (like meditating for 100 days straight).

Similarly, Bold Goals related to the giving back Pillar may be achieved in a variety of ways, with each one dependent on individual preferences and opportunities.

Regardless, everyone can benefit in their pursuit of a Bold Life by considering these overall Pillars in a broader sense. Thus, applying the information in this book from a general to a more individualized manner is encouraged.

Another important point to make regarding the Seven Pillars relates to their relative importance and your stage of life. As you evolve and grow, different Pillars will likely change in their level of priority and focus of attention.

For example, you may invest more effort in health, giving back, or relationship activities as you age due to a variety of reasons.

Career success and achievement may be a greater focus during your younger years.

These are natural developmental changes that we all experience over time. Therefore, you can recognize that you won't likely address every Pillar to the same extent throughout your lifetime. However, understanding the importance of each Pillar can serve you well as you progress along your journey.

It should also be noted that each person will not necessarily address each of the Seven Pillars throughout the course of their life. In fact, one person may completely dedicate their entire life to the Pillar of career. They may define their most meaningful goal and inspirations all within this Pillar and see little need to invest in others.

Other individuals, however, may seek a more balanced approach to a Bold Life throughout their lifetime. For them, different pursuits in different Pillars will provide greater meaning and a bolder life.

But in both instances, each can attain a Bold Life. There is no one-size-fits-all approach!

In addition to assigning different levels of importance to different Pillars, you will also likely identify specific aspects within each Pillar that offer you the most meaning. In fact, you may realize that you are already leading a Bold Life in some areas or Pillars.

In these instances, the Seven Pillars serve as sources for inspiration where you may define what provides bold meaning to you.

Here again, which aspects you choose to address within each Pillar is highly individualized based on your own personal situation and preferences. Assigning your time, energy, and other resources to the pursuits that provide you the most value and meaning is certainly recommended.

While the Seven Pillars are excellent sources of inspiration in defining areas where to invest your efforts and resources, they are not to be confused with actual goals.

For example, the Pillar of Finances might be mistaken as a goal since all of us want to have a good financial situation in life to some degree. However, this is not a goal! (We will discuss in greater detail in the next chapter.) Instead, the Finances Pillar represents simply a life category where many bold goals can be identified.

As you delve into financial concepts and define specific areas where you would like your life to be bolder, you can embrace specific Bold Goals. Thus, the Seven Pillars are simply a resource that helps inspire you to find those Bold Goals that offer the greatest meaning to you personally.

In the chapters to follow, detailed information will be provided that will better define each of the Seven Pillars. Within each of the Seven Pillars, specific considerations will be offered that can help inspire you and guide you in determining key areas that are important to you. As you will notice as you read about the different Pillars, some overlap in concepts may exist. For example, meaningful Bold Goals in your career may also involve goals related to finance. Those related to health may align with some relationship goals.

This is inevitable as well as welcome. When this occurs, it simply provides opportunities for congruence in the Bold Life activities you choose to take.

You may decide to focus on a single Pillar at a time, with each having different goals and a different set of strategies.

Alternatively, you may choose to pursue a common goal relative to two or more Pillars. For example, pursuing exotic travel with your children or with close friends can enhance the Pillars involving relationships as well as experiences.

This same integration of Bold Goals may occur when volunteer efforts are used to help others in the community. This could promote a bolder life in both the Relationships and Giving Back Pillars. And running a marathon for charity could integrate goals in the Bold Life Pillars of Giving Back and Health.

As you become increasingly more creative in your pursuit of a Bold Life, you will learn how to make the most of your time and energy through such integrations.

While integrating the activities related to meaningful goals under each of the Seven Pillars offers more efficient use of your time and energy, these integrations have other advantages as well.

By combining goals within more than one Pillar, you enjoy the opportunity for greater fulfillment, joy, and happiness in the process. The deep satisfaction that might occur by pursuing a Bold Life in one area will only be increased if combined with other ones.

In essence, such efforts provide positive reinforcement in the Bold Life process because of the exponential benefits received when you integrate more than one Pillar. This is certainly not required, and in fact, this choice is not for everyone. But for many, the effects of pursuing Bold Goals in multiple Pillars offer much more than simple additive effects.

With this overview of the Seven Pillars, the following chapter will offer important insights and approaches in identifying Bold Goals within these important areas. Unlike routine goals you may have in your life, Bold Goals are much more expansive.

Regardless of whether they are highly personalized to your situation or relative to the bold achievements of others, it is important to create truly meaningful goals that will help you realize the Bold Life you desire.

And by using the Seven Pillars as a resource of motivation and inspiration for these goals, you will soon be prepared to take action accordingly.

> *The inspiration for your Bold Goal will come within one of the Seven Pillars, but is what you consider a Bold Goal actually too broad? Don't worry, the Goal Refiner Worksheet has you covered.*

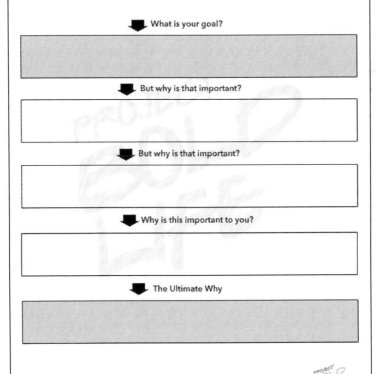

KNOW YOUR WHY
GOAL REFINER

▶ Every goal needs to be distilled down to its most basic motivation, for only in those "why" questions can true inspiration be found.

Start by putting your goal in the top box. Then move down to the box below it and answer the question "Why?" Then do it again, then again. Since the aim is to gain a better understanding of your motivations, your "Ultimate Why" will be the most distilled understanding of your goal.

What is your goal?

But why is that important?

But why is that important?

Why is this important to you?

The Ultimate Why

PBL = Pi + (S/G) + Ap

Start by putting your goal in the top box. Now answer perhaps the most important question of all when it comes to determining your Bold Goals: "Why?"

Repeat in the box below, answering that new "Why?"

Repeat again. And again.

The purpose behind this is to distill your reasoning until it becomes a truly concise—and, inevitably—more realistic thing worth achieving.

For example, let's say your stated goal is to get in shape?

Why is that your goal?

Let's say your answer to that is, "So I can be active with my kids more."

Why is that your goal?

Let's say your answer is, "So we can spend more quality time together as a family."

Can you see how refining this stated goal is making the true goal more crystallized and grounded in truth? The original goal of getting in shape, which would clearly reside in the Health Pillar, is suddenly something that belongs in the Relationships Pillar.

This kind of accuracy in goal setting will help you in successfully completing them!

Chapter 6 – The Cycle of Life and Your Bold Life Goals

"Times of transition are strenuous, but I love them. They are an opportunity to purge, rethink, prioritize, and be intentional about new habits. We can make our new normal any way we want." - Kristin Armstrong, Olympic Gold Medalist

It's no secret that change is inevitable. Despite our best efforts to create stability and consistency in our lives, life around us continues to evolve. These changes naturally require us to adapt and react, and in the process, we are forced to make specific shifts in our behaviors and pursuits. If we choose not to do so, then we often miss out on some of the precious gifts life has in store for us. And when we resist needed change, we may face stagnation, which limits our potential to live a truly bold life.

Therefore, it is clear that living a Bold Life requires us to not only tolerate change but to embrace it as a powerful force that enhances the quality of the life we can lead.

But at the same time, a natural desire for consistency and stability does exist. This desire is not necessarily a bad thing. Stability provides a foundation of strength upon which we can better predict outcomes and achieve our goals. Consistency creates the opportunity to have lasting relationships and trust with others.

However, these pursuits must be balanced with the ability to adapt and evolve as changes occur in our lives and within our environment. When we are able to achieve both consistency and adaptability in a harmonious way, then we position ourselves to truly excel.

In essence, this constant give and take between stability and change provide the background upon which we strive to be our very best. These ever-changing shifts are what define a cycle of life. It is like a beautiful dance between two partners with each occasionally taking the lead. Change may be dominant during times of transition, yet a consistent set of values and character exists underneath that provides both the strength and the purpose required. Achieving a balance between the two is what invites the greatest opportunities for excellence throughout life. And recognizing the constant state of flux that exists as this dance occurs allows us to better appreciate the cycle of life that we are experiencing.

Understanding that we all experience this cycle of life, it only makes sense that our priorities will periodically change over time. When trying to achieve a Bold Life, it is, therefore, important to recognize that our Bold Goals will evolve and change as well.

What might seem a top priority at one stage of life may not be as important at other times. Thus, we must shift our Bold Goals accordingly and determine which of the Seven Pillars are most crucial to consider as these evolutions take place. In doing so, we greatly enhance our capacity to realize a Bold Life and achieve all our Bold Goals in the process.

You've figured out which Pillars contain your greatest sources of inspiration. But which ones should you tackle first? Fear not, because the Pillar Planner Worksheet can help you.

PILLAR PLANNER

▶ What Pillars deserve attention now and what Pillars deserve attention later? By filling out which Pillars merited a "Very Important" ranking (from the Pillar Ranker worksheet) and accounting for which ones warrant immediate attention, this worksheet will help you visualize a long term plan.

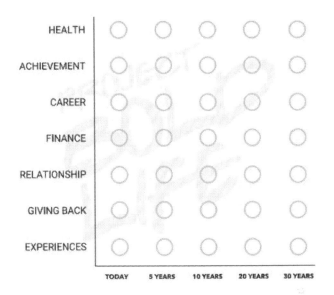

	TODAY	5 YEARS	10 YEARS	20 YEARS	30 YEARS
HEALTH	○	○	○	○	○
ACHIEVEMENT	○	○	○	○	○
CAREER	○	○	○	○	○
FINANCE	○	○	○	○	○
RELATIONSHIP	○	○	○	○	○
GIVING BACK	○	○	○	○	○
EXPERIENCES	○	○	○	○	○

$PBL = (Ti) + S/G + Ap$

The Pillar Ranker asked you to label which Pillars were "very important" to your Bold Goals. Clearly, those very important Pillars should be addressed first. But what if there are multiple goals in multiple Pillars?

Clearly, some deserve attention now and some deserve attention later, and the Pillar Planner can aid you in visualizing a timeline for all of that.

First, put an "X" within the circle that marks when you want to BEGIN striving towards achieving a particular Bold Goal within a Pillar row.

For instance, if you want to set a marathon running record in your hometown, and you want to do it now, you'd put an X in the first circle in the row for Health. That first circle is in the "Today" column.

When would you like to accomplish that goal? Within five years? Ten years?

Put an X in the corresponding column that will mark that anticipated completion of this Bold Goal. Now fill in any circles in between the beginning and endpoints and circle the entire line of Xs.

What about your goal of climbing Mount Everest? (Although that could be counted as within the Experiences or Achievement Pillars, we're just going to consider it an Achievement.) When do you want to begin striving towards that one? What about accomplishing it?

Let's say you will set out to complete it once the marathon is complete, so ten years. Put an X in that circle.

As for achieving it, let's say 20 years – put an X in that circle, and make a bigger circle encompassing the beginning and end of that goal.

Finally, you determined that you want to spend some time later in life volunteering for local charities – when, exactly?

Let's just assume that it will start 20 years from now and continue until 30 years from now (or beyond); in the row for Giving Back, mark the appropriate circles and hand-draw a circle around those.

Congrats! Now you have a visual representation of when you should tackle your separate Bold Goals and how long they will take in relation to each other.

This is helpful in a number of ways—not the least of which is that this visualization can help you determine when you will be able to tackle each and all of your Bold Goals.

After all, a good recipe for failure is to try to do everything you want to do at once.

No one has time for all of that!

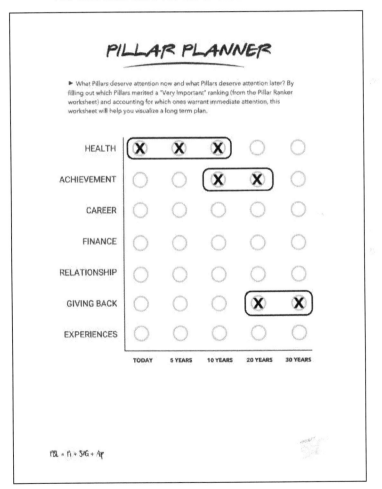

Shifting Priorities, Shifting Pillars

Human development never stops. From the time we are born until our final hours, we are constantly changing, evolving, growing, and adapting. Naturally, this includes physical changes, but similarly, it also involves our emotional outlook, social interactions, spirituality, and other aspects of our lives that make us human. Because of this, the aspects of our life that occupy our highest priorities change and evolve as well. And this affects how we pursue a Bold Life at any given time.

It doesn't matter how old you are - odds are, you can look at an early time in your life and remember when you had a vastly different set of priorities, priorities that were relevant to your age and situation then, but likely irrelevant to your age and situation now.

Maybe it was previously of the utmost importance to you to climb the corporate ladder, or spend a summer abroad, or accomplish some physical feat, or even just make the starting lineup for a high school basketball team.

But you're in a completely different place in your lifecycle now, and that different place means a new set of things that are important to you.

And those shifting priorities mean shifting goals.

In addition, through the lens of the Seven Pillars, we can see that those things that were previously important (like the aforementioned climbing of the corporate ladder, the summer abroad and the high school basketball team) can be categorized under career, experiences and health. But your shift in priorities and goals likely means new Pillars to account for.

It would be a mistake to think that a shift in priorities reflects a failure to adequately plan ahead. But that's not necessarily the case. Each of us will experience changing priorities during the course of our lives. These shifts occur simply because we are constantly adapting and changing as individuals and human beings. The cycle of life affects all of us, and the majority of us will experience changes in the Bold Goals that we pursue as we grow and evolve.

Someone in their 20s might choose to commit to the pursuit of a major health goal during their peak athletic years. Or a person may want to travel the world in an effort to achieve bold experiences and levels of achievement. For each of us, the Bold Life goals we choose will vary based on our own situation and desires. And for most of us, these goals will also shift and change as we grow.

It is perfectly acceptable, if not the norm, for our priorities and goals to change over time as we pursue a truly Bold Life. This reflects the cycle of life and the process of human development that is both continuous and ever-changing. For this reason, it is important to reassess your priorities and the most important pursuits at various times of your life. This will require self-reflection, reassessment, and taking a survey of your current situation. And to some extent, it will require determining exactly what has changed that is encouraging your priorities to shift.

By pursuing these activities, you will not only be able to redefine your Bold Goals more effectively, but also have a deeper appreciation for the value they have in your life at any given time.

Art Imitating Life – The Bold Life Edition

In season four, episode seven of the award-winning Showtime hit show "The Affair," there is an interesting interaction between Helen, played by the wonderful actress Maura Tierney, and a young pregnant woman, that highlights choices we all face as to important goals in life.

Helen is a middle-aged mother of three with children ranging between early teens and early twenties. She has been looking forward to more time for herself and her aspirations.

She is married for a second time, and her husband has terminal cancer. Helen is seeking an answer to a very important question in life.

Should she grant her dying husband's request to have a first and only child between them? He has never had children and wants one as a legacy for his parents and as a symbol of the love he and Helen share.

Helen ends up going to an overnight moonwalk with her next-door neighbor – an event where other women gather seeking inspiration and insight into their lives.

During the introspective banquet prior to the Mooncircle, Helen establishes herself as the voice of reason and experience. She is older than all the other women and provides her insight into many of the issues the younger women are concerned with. Everyone is asked to write their fears upon paper cards and give them to the Mooncircle guru, Gaelle. Helen puts in a blank card.

A young pregnant woman expresses fear about the Bold Life question – what will she do with her life when the baby arrives? On her card, she writes, "I am afraid having children is going to steal my creative spirit. I have so much more to accomplish. What if I wake up an old woman and realize I gave up all my energy to my children."

She is concerned her life, personal goals and aspirations will all come to an end once the baby comes. She is not ready to give up her dreams. The young woman appears to be at a crossroads as to which Pillars will she have to choose to focus on going forward.

After the group looks stumped, the pregnant woman continues: "I'm, like, freaking out. Like seriously now, I am not prepared for this. What if this ruins my life? This is my life."

Gaelle tells her the answer is within her and to surrender. The pregnant woman gets even more emotional and says she has no clue. She has never been pregnant before.

Helen says, "I know how it feels. And I do remember being terrified before my first daughter was born. My husband said I was acting like a caged animal."

The pregnant woman says she is a furniture designer and Helen says that she loves to design and used to have her own shop.

"Yes, your life is about to completely change," says Helen. "But not in the way you think. It doesn't get smaller. It gets larger. Right after I had my first daughter, Whitney, I had this moment and I remember it very clearly. I was looking at her little face and it suddenly occurred to me that was going to outlive me. Her life was going to extend beyond mine and I was finite. Just dust in the wind. And so I just said to myself, "Okay, if that's true, what am I going to do with my one wild and precious life?"

She further explains that you do not have to give up your life for your child. "You just have to make room for her. Or him… The heart actually does expand. I have no idea how it does it but it always seems to make room for children."

What Helen did for the pregnant woman was help her with a question every future parent faces: how to handle new child obligations and continue to live a life that includes individual dimensions and goals.

And her acknowledgment that the idea of children/family can be terrifying helps frame for everyone what truly dealing with any of the Seven Pillars can be like. Each Pillar upon introspection is important, and we only live one life.

Will you be all you can be in your career? All you can be to your family? Financially? Will you experience and see all you can see?

Helen's insight that the heart actually does expand can be applied to your Bold Life. You can expand your thinking, your heart and your approach to make room. You may not be able to focus on all the Pillars at the same time, yet you can "make room" for what is important to you.

Understanding Cycle of Life Shifts

When it comes to the changes in our priorities, a number of influences and events may trigger these shifts. For many, the natural evolution of life's stages accounts for changes in what we find as most important. Physical changes that occur with age, changes in social or career roles, changing family structures and dynamics, and advancing emotional maturity are examples of these natural changes that occur throughout a person's lifespan.

Therefore, it's no surprise that we will tend to focus on different Pillars and goals over time.

While these natural transitions of life affect our focus and priorities, other events may also do the same, but more abruptly. A sudden and unexpected diagnosis with a major health condition may encourage a change in Bold Goals to pursue health and relationships more fully.

Or a person who has lost all their possessions in an unfortunate tragedy may be focused on their finances or on giving back to others based on their experiences. In essence, Bold Goals can change for a variety of reasons, and the change may be sudden or gradual in nature.

Priorities can shift for a variety of reasons. It is not uncommon as we mature and gain a sense of community and social responsibility to value different things. But this same shift may have occurred much earlier in life for others based on different dreams, interests, and experiences. Understanding this, one person may choose to pursue a single Bold Life Pillar their entire life, while others may pursue all of them at once.

Without question, we all experience a cycle of life that affects our perspectives, but how we interpret these changes and their relationship to our view of a Bold Life is truly unique.

It should also be stressed that a Bold Goal is not one that can be defined in a vacuum. In other words, pursuing a career in law may be bold for some and not for others.

In fact, it may be impossible for many for a number of reasons. Bold Goals must be interpreted based on a person's unique situation as well as their personal interests, dreams, and past experiences.

And they must be interpreted based on the life stage they are currently experiencing.

All of these factors must be taken into account when determining which of the Seven Pillars and Bold Goals are among your top priorities.

Finding the Balance for the Boldest Life

When it comes to realizing a truly Bold Life, finding a balance between consistency and change is essential. Some things need to remain stable to serve as a foundation and source of strength and focus. These might include your core values, overarching life dreams, and even your personal philosophical beliefs. But at the same time, embracing change and being willing to adapt and evolve is also important. These aspects are inevitable as a part of life, but they are also critical for leading a Bold Life because they incite growth and achievement.

Part of finding this important balance is appreciating the cycle of life and the changing priorities that occur along the way. At different times, you will have different priorities as it relates to your pursuit of a Bold Life. And because of this, you will likely select different Pillars in choosing specific goals to pursue during these different phases. This insight is important to understand because it encourages you to alter your course at times when a shift is needed. And in doing so, you can optimize your efforts and the use of the resources available to you to embody the boldest life possible.

Life takes us all on a journey that is unique and highly individualized. Therefore, it is not possible to predict what Bold Goals might be best for any particular person at any given time. Instead, you must invest energy and time into determining your own personal Bold Goals based on your own dreams, desires, interests, and life situation. Only you can correctly determine if the life you are pursuing is truly a Bold Life.

With this in mind, the next step is to select which Bold Goals you want to achieve. Using the Seven Pillars as guides, you can select the boldest goals possible to help you realize a life full of satisfaction and fulfillment. The following chapter will help you do just that. By appreciating how to best choose Bold Goals, you can plan a roadmap to your ultimate successes in life.

And with an appreciation of the changes that occur throughout the cycle of life, you can revisit these same goals and consider new ones along the way.

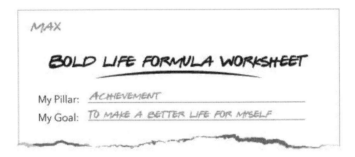

The 16-year-old boy, Max, had a small bag with two changes of clothes and a winter jacket in his hand. It was 1906. He was about to embark on a journey that would alter his life forever. He looked his mother and father in the eyes and tearfully said goodbye. At the time, he did not know that he would never see or speak with his parents again.

Max's father, Michael, had sold their prized white horse in order to give Max money to embark on his journey. Michael was sacrificing his family's wealth in hard times so that Max could leave and have a life of opportunity.

Max's country had been war-torn for years. Most people in his community were barely surviving. He was small for his age but strong. He knew he would have to muster all his strength to successfully navigate what was ahead.

His Bold Goal was to travel to the United States-- a land of far greater opportunity than what his own country offered him--and work hard for a better life.

But the first obstacle Max faced was an over 700- mile long journey from his hometown, Bachów, Rushistan (in what is now known as Poland) to Hamburg, Germany.

He would do it by foot, hitching horse-pulled cart rides and catching some fourth-class train travel.

It would not be an easy first journey. He knew he would need to stop numerous times and try to find some day work.

He would need to earn enough for food and a place to sleep so that he would not have to use the money reserved for his Hamburg-to-America ship travel.

It promised to be a difficult, arduous undertaking, and there were no guarantees of success. But Max was determined to seek out that Bold Life he knew was worth fighting for, so off he went...

Max's bold undertaking began well over a century before the design of any of the Project Bold Life Worksheets. But we can certainly frame his inspiration through the Pillars and his prioritization through the Pillar Ranker.

What drove Max to leave his home was a strong desire to change his life—both in terms of finances and job (he also wanted to someday have a family, but that part of his story will come later). Therefore, Max would've ranked Finances and Career as "Very Important". Everything else took a backseat to those two sources of inspiration.

MAX

PILLAR RANKER

	IMPORTANCE	TIMING	WHY
HEALTH	○ Very Important ○ Important ☑ Not Important	○ Now ○ Later ☑ Much Later	_____ _____ _____
FINANCES	☑ Very Important ○ Important ○ Not Important	☑ Now ○ Later ○ Much Later	*FINDING A BETTER* *LIFE WITH MORE* *OPPORTUNITIES IS CRUCIAL*
CAREER	☑ Very Important ○ Important ○ Not Important	☑ Now ○ Later ○ Much Later	*GREATER JOB OPPORTUNITIES* *& HARD WORK WILL MEAN* *A BETTER LIFE*
ACHIEVEMENTS	○ Very Important ○ Important ☑ Not Important	○ Now ○ Later ☑ Much Later	_____ _____ _____
RELATIONSHIPS	○ Very Important ☑ Important ○ Not Important	○ Now ☑ Later ○ Much Later	*STARTING A FAMILY* *IS IMPORTANT*
GIVING BACK	○ Very Important ○ Important ☑ Not Important	○ Now ○ Later ☑ Much Later	_____ _____ _____
EXPERIENCES	○ Very Important ○ Important ☑ Not Important	○ Now ○ Later ☑ Much Later	_____ _____ _____

- HEALTH — Both physical and mental well-being
- FINANCES — The fiscal wherewithal to survive and thrive
- CAREER — Work that fulfills
- ACHIEVEMENTS — Accomplishments you are proud of
- RELATIONSHIPS — Family, friends and everything in between
- GIVING BACK — Charity and volunteering;
- EXPERIENCES — Those memorable things that make life worth living

IMPORTANCE
VI - Very Important   I - Important

TIMING
Now   Later   Much Later

PBL = (Pi) + S²G + Ap

PROJECT BOLD LIFE

Chapter 7 – Defining Bold Goals

"I bought a piano once because I had the dream of playing 'As Time Goes By' as some girl's leaning on it drinking a martini. Great image. But none of it worked out. I can't even play chopsticks. But I've got a nice piano at my house."- George Clooney

Most people would have little trouble defining goals in their lives. Some would say their goal is to be successful. That's a great aspiration, but what does it actually mean?

Others might reply that their goal is to be a good spouse and parent. Again, this is another great concept, but is this really a well-defined goal? In actuality, no. Because they lack specificity, these are not true goals. Success to one person will not define success for another. And what it means to be a good parent can certainly have a wide range of perspectives. Thus, not only must goals identify a future desire, but they must also be specific enough to guide action.

For many people, their goals are not really goals. They are contemplative aspirations, wishes, or dreams for the future. It's great to dream and wonder about life's possibilities, but many aspirations will simply never happen without a more specific plan of action and target. Some people think they want to be scratch golfers or run a competitive marathon. Some people want to be the CEO of their own company. Others may want to go to medical school and perform groundbreaking cancer research. These are definitely "bold" ideas. They are real and inspiring. But are they important enough to you to justify the effort it will take to achieve them?

Being able to determine what is a true goal for you and what is simply a wish is very important in your pursuit of a Bold Life.

Suppose you would like to quit smoking. Based on surveys, around 46 million smokers in the U.S. say they would like to kick this habit. However, the actual success rate varies greatly depending on the actions taken. For those who never enroll in a smoking cessation program, the success rate is roughly five percent. But for those who put their energies into this type of program, success rates can be as high as 40 percent. The former group of tobacco smokers simply "hope" to quit, but the latter group made quitting an actual goal.

When it comes to Bold Goals, one of the first questions to ask yourself is what is most important to you in your life. Often, people's response might be something like, "My family," or "My kids." These are certainly important, but **what** about your family or children is important to you?

Your next response might be, "I want my children to be successful." Again, this is also a valued goal, but **how** do you define success for your children? Ultimately, the actual answer at the end of a series of such questions arrives at the specific goal to be considered.

Perhaps, the goal is for your children to complete graduate school and earn a six-figure salary. Or maybe you want them to grow up to be moral, responsible adults and be a pillar in their community. In both cases, the goals provide a more specific and tangible target.

For any goal, including Bold Goals, you have to move your thinking from the conceptual to the specific. Like an onion, you have to peel back the successive layers until you arrive at the precise target that most accurately defines the goal. In performing this exercise, you accomplish two very important tasks. The first requires you to seriously reflect on what you truly value as part of your life goals. The second establishes goals with enough precision that an Action Plan can be devised. Without these two very important steps, the chance any goal will be successfully attained drops significantly.

From this perspective, the first step in determining how to pursue a Bold Life is to identify actual goals to be considered. Using the Seven Pillars as a source of inspiration, an array of life goals may be chosen. But in each case, goals must be more than a conceptual idea. They must be specific. They have to be precise enough to direct your actions so that the actual goal can be attained. And as we will discuss next, they must also be SMART!

The "SMART" Way to Determine Your Bold Life Goals

Making your Bold Goals specific is an essential part of goal setting. Being precise in how you define those things you value the most allows you to better guide your efforts and actions accordingly. But being specific in your goals is only one key feature of an effective goal. Several others exist, and they are summarized in the acronym "SMART." Not only should your goals be Specific, but they should also be Measurable, Attainable, Relevant, and Time-Bound.

Let's break this down a bit. We have covered what it means to make your Bold Goals specific. And to a significant degree, this allows your goals to also be measurable.

For example, suppose one of your Bold Goals is to run a marathon. This goal is specific, and if you succeed in running a marathon, attaining your goal is certainly measurable. But you could take this a step further.

Suppose you not only wanted to run a marathon, but also complete it within four hours. Or perhaps you might want to run the marathon fast enough to qualify for the Boston Marathon. All of these goals are specific and measurable, but they demonstrate how greater specificity goes hand-in-hand with greater precision in measuring success.

Being able to measure whether or not you achieved a goal is an important characteristic of any goal. After all, it's of little use to establish a goal that fails to have standards by which your efforts can be evaluated. Measurements provide a sense of accomplishment and motivate us in our pursuits. This highlights another important consideration when it comes to making sure that attaining your goals can be measured. The best goals are those whose completion can not only be quantified but whose progress can be tracked as well.

By defining a series of measurements that show progress toward your ultimate goal, you fuel your motivation to an even greater extent. These "micro-wins" along the way help keep you focused and ensure you are moving in the right direction. For the marathoner, this may mean setting a series of progressive goals in the number of miles run per week. In doing so, efforts can be tracked and measured over time, and if needed, adjustments can be made to better ensure success in attaining the final goal of running the marathon.

Of course, every goal may not be an attainable one. Not everyone is able to run a marathon, or even a 5K for that matter. Many dream of being a professional basketball player in the NBA, but is this realistic for the vast majority? Certainly not. Thus, while effective goals need to be specific and measurable, they also need to be attainable. Goals that fail to be achievable and realistic can actually undermine our motivation. Despite our efforts, progress isn't made, and this ultimately affects self-confidence and enthusiasm.

Thankfully, realistic goals offer just the opposite. We become empowered as we see actual progress resulting from our efforts and investments. When we choose goals that are attainable, we invite a higher level of excitement and motivation toward our pursuits. As we will discuss, this doesn't mean goals shouldn't challenge us and demand some level of struggle. But making sure the Bold Goals you choose are truly possible to attain is similarly important to foster success.

At first glance, the attainability of a goal and its realistic nature appears to be the same thing. After all, if a goal is not attainable, then it is not going to be realistic, either. While this is true, the opposite may not be. In other words, a goal may be attainable but not realistic. What's the difference?

The key distinction involves ability versus feasibility. For a goal to be actually attainable, we need to have the basic skills, talents, and abilities to achieve that goal. For the person aspiring to play in the NBA, they must have the height, agility, accuracy and talent to even consider attaining this goal. If not, then their dream of playing professional basketball is not attainable no matter how badly they want it.

In contrast, a realistic goal is one that is feasible given the other goals, resources, and constraints that exist in your life. For example, you might have the raw skills and talent to compete within the NBA with the proper commitment and training. But your capacity to invest the time, energy and dedication to this pursuit simply isn't feasible. Perhaps you have other priorities that would interfere, or maybe you simply don't have the level of desire for this particular goal to make it a reality. Regardless, in these situations, the goal of playing in the NBA is completely attainable, yet it is not realistic given your circumstances.

This distinction between attainable and realistic is what determines whether a specific goal is relevant to you. Relevance means that your pursuits offer value and importance to you personally. In addition to being something that you could achieve, SMART goals must also impart meaning to you and your life. When this exists, your goals will have inherent relevance and be a priority for you. And when a goal becomes a priority, it becomes increasingly more likely and realistic that you will succeed in attaining that goal.

Lastly, SMART goal setting requires placing some time constraints on attaining a goal. Consider the person who dreams of opening their own business. Day after day, they continue to work for a local hospital while telling friends and family their plans to eventually open their own community recreation center. Is the goal specific and measurable? It would seem so. Is it attainable and realistic? Possibly. But without a timetable, the chance the goal will be attained diminishes rapidly. Why? Simply because the goal lacks accountability for completion. Without a specific timeframe by which a goal should be achieved, efforts in attaining the goal often lack enough commitment.

By establishing a timeframe for a goal to be achieved, you make your efforts more measurable in nature. But at the same time, you also draw a line in the sand that holds you accountable for attaining that goal in a reasonable amount of time. Rather than floundering or procrastinating in your pursuits, you instead become motivated to act knowing a deadline exists.

And by letting others know your timetable for achieving your goals, you enhance this accountability factor even more.

Without question, having a set time by which a goal should be achieved is an important feature of effective goal setting. With a set time, you will increase your chances of success greatly.

In terms of Bold Goals, using the SMART approach to goal setting can help get you off on the right foot. While the Seven Pillars serve as sources of inspiration for meaningful goals in your life, effective goal setting strategies must also be used to increase your chances for success. But Bold Goals require more than simply using a strategy for defining key aspects of the targets you want to pursue. Bold Goals actually demand you stretch and expand yourself in defining these goals so you may lead the boldest life possible.

Every Bold Goal undertaking has an upside. But the reality is, there may be a downside as well—one that could involve time and resources being taken away from other aspects of your life.

Therefore, it's always important to do a cost/benefit analysis before setting off on your path up Bold Mountain.

Thankfully, the Bold Goals: Pros vs. Cons Worksheet can help you.

BOLD GOALS

PROS VS. CONS

▶ The execution of any Bold Goal will have an upside and a downside, both as they affect you and affect the world around you. Use this Pro vs. Con sheet to determine the cost/benefit analysis of your potential Bold undertaking.

My Bold Goal is _____

Self Pros	Self Cons
1.	1.
2.	2.
3.	3.
4.	4.
5.	5.
External Pros	**External Cons**
1.	1.
2.	2.
3.	3.
4.	4.
5.	5.

PBL = PI + SPG + AP

There will be personal pros and cons that affect you, and there will be external pros and cons that affect those around you.

List them all in the appropriate boxes.

For example, let's say you want to retire at 33 like the McCurry Family. The "Self Cons" will of course include living frugally, but those Self Cons will most certainly affect your family as well, *thereby making them important things to list as "External Cons".*

The purpose of this Worksheet is to put down in writing the true cost of tackling your Bold Goal and determine if it's actually worth it... and to make sure all parties who might be affected are on board.

Making Goals Stretch and Inspirational

For many, the key to living a Bold Life comes down to doing some deeper work as it relates to goals. Goals can be motivating, de-motivating or inspirational. Setting smart goals that inspire is not hard. It takes some thought. Some creativity. Let me give an example.

Suppose you are just starting college. If Achievement is an important Pillar and your education is important, then an inspiring goal could make a huge difference. Your goal could be ordinary or bold, depending on your approach. An ordinary goal might look like: "My goal is to just graduate." Pretty ordinary, right! How might you make this Pillar of Achievement more stretch? More bold? More inspiring?

You could set a different goal. Maybe a goal to be on the Dean's List every year? Dean's List with Distinction? Or maybe it's graduation with Distinction? Cum laude? Magna cum laude? Summa cum laude? You could choose to double major or to take advanced Master's degree classes as an undergraduate, no? Set a goal to be recognized as the top student in your field of study at your school? As you can see, all of these would be more inspiring than "My goal is to just graduate."

Here is a list of some common categories for goal setting and their acronyms. They can be very useful for inspirational goal-setting.

Intrinsic
- **PB- Personal Best**

Extrinsic
- **FR- Family Record**
- **TR- Town Record**
- **CR- County Record**
- **SR- State Record**
- **NR- National Record**
- **WR- World Record**
- **OR- Olympic Record**
- **GOAT- Greatest of All Time**

"Personal Best" is a very common inspiring dimension. It is part of an important driver of success for goals. Intrinsic goals are inherently more deeply personal. Intrinsic inspiration can result in a stronger connection and commitment to the work necessary to achieve your goals.

"Family Records" can be particularly motivating and bold. First in family to graduate high school, college or to get an advanced degree are examples. First in family to buy a house or become a vice president at a company is another example. First in family to become a doctor, lawyer, nurse or other professional… these are all examples of inspiring bold goals.

And you do not always need to be best or first to make an inspiring goal come alive for you.

"Personal Records" as well as "Extrinsic Records" can also be made inspiring by tiering measurements or percentage rankings. For example, setting a goal of graduating in the top 10% of your class is bold. For many, a top 10% goal may be more inspiring as it will be viewed as more achievable and keep a person motivated and working towards their goal.

Tiering concepts apply to many areas of goal setting.

Financial goals can be particularly inspiring when this idea is applied. Shooting for an income goal is a good example of this.

According to the 2017 Social Security records, one must earn $118,400 to be in the top 10% of income in the United States. To be in the top 5%, you must earn $299,810.[11] Another bold goal could be to own your home free and clear of any mortgage. Only 37% of people in the U.S. own their home free and clear, with most owners being over 70 years of age. Nowadays, 15.6% of millennials own a home free and clear. An inspiring goal, therefore, could be to own your home free and clear by a certain age.

Ultimately, the purpose behind this intrinsic vs. extrinsic goal discussion is to point out that anyone—ANYONE—can set Bold Goals for themselves. Whether

---

[11] https://www.investopedia.com/personal-finance/how-much-income-puts-you-top-1-5-10/

you're setting out to beat a personal best or become the best in the world, it's all bold if you stretch yourself.

By forcing you to stretch and expand ideas about the level of success you want in your life, Bold Goals will naturally demand the most of you. The key to defining a Bold Goal for you will depend upon whether the endeavor you want to pursue requires you to go above and beyond to attain something special.

If you think about Bold Goals as stretch goals, you can appreciate their importance to a Bold Life.

Whenever we choose to stretch ourselves in new directions and embrace new challenges, we naturally invite the opportunity to grow and expand. In essence, this is what it means to pursue a Bold Life. Without growth, we never realize the opportunity to improve and experience a life that embodies excellence. For this reason, Bold Goals should be those that challenge us and demand change while pursuing greater meaning from our life.

In considering Bold Goals further, the actual goal itself does not define boldness alone. Whether or not a goal stretches you beyond your comfort zone will depend on your circumstances. In other words, context matters!

For example, choosing to become a nurse practitioner at 25 years of age may not necessarily be a Bold Goal for many. But making this a goal at the age of 60 years of age may certainly be. Likewise, attaining a college education may seem commonplace for thousands of individuals. But it could be one of the boldest goals conceivable for a mother of five children who would be the first in her family to graduate from college.

Want another example of a stretch goal? Let's revisit Max.

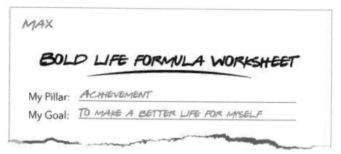

MAX

BOLD LIFE FORMULA WORKSHEET

My Pillar: *ACHIEVEMENT*

My Goal: *TO MAKE A BETTER LIFE FOR MYSELF*

Once he arrived in Hamburg, Max needed to procure passage for a ship. The ship he settled upon was the SS Patricia. Built in 1899, the SS Patricia was a transatlantic steamship owned by the Hamburg America Line. It had four decks and could hold 2,500 passengers.
Max bought the least expensive passage fare, steerage. Approximately 2,100 of the 2,500 passengers would travel in steerage, packed in like cattle. His ticket would cost about $30, which was a fortune back then. This was the lowest part of the boat.

Steerage conditions in the early 1900s were atrocious. A steamship trip across the Atlantic in 1906 typically took six to ten days. In a seminal book, "On the Trail of The Immigrant", by Edward

A. Steiner and published in 1906[12], the difficulty of steerage ship travel was told to the world. Steiner, who in 1905 went undercover and travelled steerage to understand the plight of the immigrant, wrote:

"The **steerage ought to be and could be abolished by law.** It is true that the Italian and Polish peasant may not be accustomed to better things at home and might not be happier in better surroundings nor know how to use them; but **it is a bad introduction to our life to treat him like an animal when he is coming to us.** He ought to be made to feel immediately, that the standard of living in America is higher than it is abroad, and that life on the higher plane begins on board of a ship. Every cabin passenger who has seen and smelt the steerage from afar, knows that **it is often indecent and inhuman;** and **I, who have lived in it, know that it is both of these and cruel besides."** (Emphasis added.) Steiner lived in Max's ship travel shoes and his eloquent reporting led work to legislation changing the conditions after 1910.

Max's trip was not easy. The SS Patricia embarked from Hamburg on July 7, 1906, and arrived in New York on July 20, 1906. Max was out to sea for 13 days. The extra length of travel meant two things: first, Max had to endure unhealthy animal-like conditions for a longer period. But more importantly, the ship hit bad weather that made the trip longer. Rough seas increased sickness and made conditions even more difficult. This was not inconsequential, as the arrival in New York would have some additional serious challenges. Could Max stay healthy enough to get in? After all, at Ellis Island,

---

[12] Edward A. Steiner, *On the Trail of the Immigrant* (Revell, 1906)

those deemed "unhealthy" were usually sent back to where they came from!

Chapter 8 - Creating Meaningful Change

"You must be the change you wish to see in the world." – Mahatma Gandhi

Change is inevitable. Nothing stays constant, and no matter how much we may dislike it at times, it is an essential aspect of life. But change for the sake of change is not necessarily ideal. Instead, real progress and growth occur when change is intentional and directed toward a positive transition and goal. That doesn't mean that the change will be without challenges, discomfort, and setbacks. But it does mean that ideal change is one that results in greater value and meaning over time.

When considering a Bold Life, change is an essential aspect that facilitates realizing Bold Goals and achievements. If we choose to remain stagnant and protect the present, by definition, we are not pursuing the boldest life possible. These types of goals fail to stretch our limits and challenge us. Such goals also squander our potential while suppressing progress. Therefore, the pursuit of a truly Bold Life acknowledges that changes will be required in order for us to add greater value and meaning to our lives.

In essence, pursuing a Bold Life demands seeking meaningful change as we grow. But what is meaningful change?

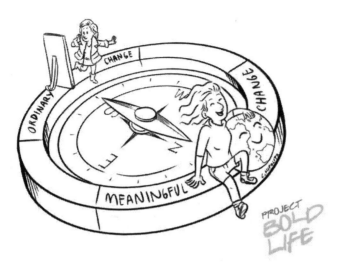

From a basic point of view, meaningful change is simply a change that adds meaning. But for a Bold Life, meaningful change should extend beyond this. After all, small goals may offer meaning or value in some regard. But for a truly Bold Life, meaningful change should be connected to some greater purpose in your life. Meaningful change should help you attain your most valued missions in life. And it should create a substantial, positive impact - not only in your life but in the lives of others.

Understanding this, the end-results of a meaningful change define the goals and targets in your Bold Life pursuits.

At the same time, the process by which change will occur should also add meaning to your life. In many instances, the journey of change offers many lessons and insights that can enhance your life. At times, these lessons and experiences may be more powerful than the ultimate achievement. Thus, how you go about meaningful changes in your life is just as important as the valued goals you choose.

Meaningful change is something that demands reflection and deep consideration. What represents meaningful change in your life? If we want to grow, learn, and realize our potential, then we acknowledge that change is necessary. But at the same time, we can also be very intentional about how we change and the meaning these decisions have. For this reason, once you have identified which Bold Goals offer you the greatest value, you must also consider how you wish to pursue these goals.

Ultimately, this means you will have to choose to change and take action accordingly.

The Science of Change: The Data Behind the Methodology

John Norcross is a Distinguished Professor of Psychology at the University of Scranton in Pennsylvania. Professor Norcross has dedicated 30 years of his life to research, writing and applying his findings on change and self-help. He is the author of over 400 publications and 20 books and has devoted his professional life to studying how people can make effective changes in their lives.

He is a board-certified specialist in psychotherapy, behavior change and self-help. In his well-researched book on behavior change, *Changeology: 5 Steps to Realizing Your Goals and Resolutions*, Norcross lays out the science and blueprint for change.

From Changeology: "The science speaks for itself: thousands of people have successfully overcome their problematic behaviors on their own with the system outlined in this book. In fact, a whopping 90 percent of people who stop smoking and 90 percent of people who gain control of problem drinking do so without formal treatment... Here's what I want to scream from the rooftops: 'There's no need to rely anymore on folk myths and grandma's advice about improving your life. We now possess compelling scientific research that can guide your behavioral metamorphosis. Let science help you; let us show you the way!"

The science of accomplishing a Bold Life is based on this same science. Self-help based upon scientific principles is typically all that is needed.

Norcross points out that change can be applied to many dimensions of life. He says that the principles apply to "bad habits, new goals, relationship improvements and life fulfillment." All of these will be part of your plan to build a Bold Life.

A second key part of Norcross's research applies to how people set and manage goals and when they do them. Norcross outlines five steps to change that require 90 days of follow-through. Those five steps are:

Psych→Prep→Perspire→Persevere→Persist[13]

It is not good enough to just pick a Bold Goal and go into action. (Perspire is defined as the action phase by Norcross.)

The "Just Do It" mentality is simply a wrong approach!

You heard that right. This is counter to many people's instincts when they make resolutions. It is also the reason so many resolutions fail. As a matter of fact, science shows that you are less likely to succeed if you eliminate the first two steps, Psych and Prep, prior to action. The first two steps should be done before going into action. The science shows they significantly increase your chances of success.

Here is some of the research and science on the importance of following the steps.

In a study titled "Processes of change in smoking cessation: A cross-validation study in cardiac patients," published by Ockene, Ockene and Kristellar in 1992 in the Journal of Substance Abuse[14], cardiac patients were monitored for the first time as to their stages of change.

---

[13] John C. Norcross, Ph.D., *Changeology: 5 Steps to Realizing Your Goals and Resolutions* (New York, Simon & Schuster, 2013)
[14] https://pubmed.ncbi.nlm.nih.gov/1458044/

From the paper's abstract: "These results are the first to support the validity of the stages and processes-of-change model of smoking cessation in a population experiencing severe illness."

Ultimately. 76% of the patients who reached Step 3 achieved success, whereas 25% of those in Step 1 managed to quit. The success differential is significant.

Norcross also examined New Year's Resolutions. He set up two groups, the "Resolvers" and the "Non-Resolvers."

The Resolvers would follow the steps and follow all of the suggested exercises prior to going into action.

The Non-Resolvers were significantly less successful at all time points across the first six months.

The Resolvers at month six were ten times more successful than the Non-Resolvers, 44% vs 4%. The data showed that "each step you take nearly doubles the probability of your long-term success."

According to all of this research, there is a hard truth to be acknowledged: **Each step you take increases your likelihood of success.**

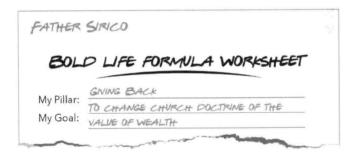

Father Robert Sirico was determined to give back to society, but his mission was unique: to educate world leaders on the morality of markets to serve the poor. While much of the clergy has long sought to redistribute wealth to help those less fortunate, he instead saw the positive impact

business had on the greater moral good. I met Father Sirico through Kris Mauren.

It was spring of 2008 and I walked into the restaurant for an early dinner prior to an event that I would be moderating in Manhattan. I was meeting the panelists I would be interviewing for the event. Dinner would provide an opportunity to get comfortable with each other and prepare before going on stage. For the first time, the film "Call of the Entrepreneur" - which was produced by the Acton Media group of the Acton Institute - would be shown to the New York City market.[15] My dinner companions/panelists all appeared in the film and we would do a "discuss the film" segment after the showing. We were expecting a crowd of several hundred businessmen, academicians, students and other media.

The first person who arrived was George Gilder. Conversations with George are never dull. George, for those who do not know him, is a very, very accomplished man. He has authored 19 books. His most famous, "Wealth and Poverty", contributed significantly to economic thinking and is one of the most famous and read books about economics of all time.[16] It sold more than one million copies since it was first published and has influenced leaders and policymakers around the world for years. The book takes on the age old important topic of decreasing poverty while increasing prosperity. It is a classic! In his early years, George was a speechwriter for political leaders, including George Romney, Richard

---

[15] To see the trailer and gain access to the full movie *Call of the Entrepreneur*, go to https://www.acton.org/films/call-of-the-entrepreneur

[16] *Wealth and Poverty: A New Edition for the Twenty-First Century* (Gateway Editions, 2012)

Nixon and Nelson Rockefeller. He was the most quoted person by President Ronald Reagan, according to a study of his presidential speeches. He is also considered one of the country's leading futurists and a technology visionary. Many of his other books deal with important technology topics. George currently serves as Chairman of Gilder Publishing LLC, located in Great Barrington, MA. He is a co-founder of the Discovery Institute.

George and I discussed a number of topics while waiting for Father Robert Sirico, one of the founders of Acton, the group behind the film. Our conversation hit a lot of topics quickly, including the film, economics, philosophy and the role of faith and god in the world of business and life. George was very clearly an expert and insightful about the topic of entrepreneurship, yet what intrigued me was George's enthusiasm for the work of Father Sirico. Father Sirico had dedicated most of his life educating people and clergy about faith's important compatibility with individual freedom, free markets and business. According to George, Father Sirico was the real rock star for this event and his work was of monumental importance. This event was part of Father Sirico's Action Plan for his Bold Goal. I was well aware of Father Sirico's work, yet I appreciated George's intellectual humility on the topic for the evening's interviews. I knew Father Sirico would be a powerful presence and influence on stage. I was looking forward to his arrival and the evening ahead...

Strategies of Success for Meaningful Change

Despite change being everywhere and constant, choosing to implement change in your life can be incredibly hard!

Think about the millions of people who attempt dieting to lose weight each year. More than half will fail in their attempt. The same goes for those taking the leap of faith and going "cold turkey" to quit smoking. And similarly, thousands of people will sign up for a gym membership as part of their New Year's resolution and never go more than a few times. Clearly, change isn't as easy as it seems.

There's a difference between change and meaningful change. In the examples just provided, meaningful change is being sought in an effort to be fitter and healthier. This differs significantly from change that is forced upon us due to unforeseen circumstances. In the former, we have to make purposeful and intentional choices to guide the change, so a valued outcome is realized. In the latter, we are simply affected by the forces of change that are requiring us to either make a choice to adapt or to resist. Both can result in positive changes in our lives, and both types of change require specific strategies in order to succeed. But only meaningful goals are intentional and guide our best efforts toward a Bold Life.

With this in mind, a number of change models have been studied and suggested over time. Kurt Lewin proposed a three-step model where we experience a process of unfreezing, changing, and refreezing. In other words, Lewin believed we had to let go of current habits, choose to behave differently, and then adopt new behaviors as new habits for success. This model offers a great perspective when considering how we can make a meaningful change. But at the same time, it can be too simplistic in providing a specific approach. This is especially true when choosing to make changes associated with your new Bold Life pursuits.

A better model of change, and one that has been studied in greater depth, was proposed by John Norcross, Carlo DiClemente, and James Prochaska. Though their original change model described six steps to realize effective and meaningful change, four of these steps are the most critical. These steps include psychologically acknowledging the need for a change, preparing for the change, taking action, and then using strategies to help you persevere and persist in your efforts. The research from their studies showed that each of these steps is incredibly important if actual change is to occur.

Why do you think so many people fail in their efforts to diet or quit smoking? Certainly, these are difficult tasks, and many barriers to success may exist. But the most significant reason failure rates are so high is because people often skip a few of the essential steps of change.

For example, when someone chooses to quit smoking cold turkey, rarely have they mentally prepared themselves or planned for the challenges they will face. As a result, they jump into action and commit to complete abstinence. But after a while, their willpower diminishes, temptations mount, and they find themselves once again smoking.

To highlight this effect, Norcross conducted an experiment among people making New Year's resolutions.[17] He compared the success rates between people who spent time mentally considering their resolution, planned out how they would achieve it, and then implemented a plan of action with those who simply acted on their resolution without any significant preparation. The results of his experiment showed that those who went through all the necessary steps for change were ten times more likely to achieve their New Year's resolution!

When considering meaningful changes in your life, it is therefore essential that the appropriate steps be taken to improve your ultimate chances of success. That means defining what types of changes provide true value and meaning to your life. By establishing your Bold Life priorities, you begin to appreciate why these goals are

---

[17] https://pubmed.ncbi.nlm.nih.gov/2980864/

important to you. This inherently starts preparing you psychologically for the needed changes to follow.

This is then followed by a planning step where you strive to remove potential obstacles while including things that might help you succeed. In other words, you start paving the way for change. With these two very important steps, your chances for change success rises tremendously.

Of course, pulling the trigger and implementing the change process is important as well, but only after you have laid the necessary groundwork.

All of these steps must be considered when pursuing an important change in your life. So, it makes sense that these steps would also be important when embarking on your journey toward a bolder and better life.

And you can rest assured that these strategies are the ones that will be highlighted and encouraged throughout this book.

Revisiting the Bold Life Formula

At this point, we have covered the key essentials needed in defining your Bold Life goals and how you should consider their pursuit. The topics discussed have outlined the process by which you can:

1. Define what a Bold Life means to you
2. Identify important priorities that impart meaning and value to your life
3. Establish the necessary groundwork required to pursue these goals.

In summary, the Bold Life Formula offers an overview of this process that you can repeatedly use as a guide in your pursuits of a Bold Life.

In considering the Bold Life Formula, let's revisit each of the three components in an effort to stress the key elements of each and their importance.

$$PBL = Pi + S^2G + Ap$$

The first component ("Pi") involves establishing meaningful goals for your life. Remember, the Seven Pillars provide sources of inspiration to help you in defining these meaningful goals. It has been shown repeatedly that all meaningful goals can be placed within one of these Pillars (if not more than one). Thus, by considering the Seven Pillars, you can be inspired and identify areas of your life where you wish to be bolder.

As discussed in this chapter, a meaningful goal is more than simply a routine accomplishment or achievement. Likewise, meaningful goals will vary from person to person based on their skills and abilities, as well as their circumstances. Meaningful goals may also be relative in nature based on the accomplishments of others or unique to you. In any case, a meaningful goal adds significant value to your life and is highly personal in nature. And by using the Seven Pillars as a resource, you can best define the meaningful goals that are a top priority for you at any given time.

In the next section of this book, each of the Seven Pillars will be discussed in detail.

In addition to better defining what each Pillar represents, this information will also serve to help inspire and motivate you in determining which Bold Goals you wish to pursue. The inspiring stories in these chapters, along with examples of what others have defined as meaningful goals, will help guide you in your efforts to define your own Bold Goals. And notably, these stories and examples can be revisited time and time again to help you periodically reassess where your current priorities lie.

Defining meaningful goals is a critical step in your pursuit of a Bold Life. But it is the second component that truly adds boldness to your efforts. The stretch component of the Bold Life Formula ("S²G") highlights the importance of stretching and expanding your pursuits in being the boldest they can be.

This step requires that you dig deep and define specifics about your goals so that they truly create a Bold Life and achieve a deeper meaning for you personally. In doing so, you invite excellence to come into your life and into the lives of others.

By stretching your meaningful goals into the boldest pursuits possible, you can better realize your full potential in life. This part of the Bold Life Formula is like a shot of steroids, taking your meaningful goals to the next level.

Likewise, by defining more detailed specifics about your goals, you become more likely to create key targets that offer the most value and meaning possible to you.

And lastly, by applying SMART goal setting strategies, you boost your chances of success even further.

Finally, in order to truly realize your boldest life possible, you must act toward the pursuit of your Bold Goals. As previously noted, however, simply jumping in with both feet without preparation is often doomed for failure. As a result, the third component of the Bold Life Formula is the creation of an Action Plan ("Ap") that will facilitate your success in attaining your Bold Goals.

This essential aspect of the formula will better ensure that you are ready to take on the challenges that come while helping you persevere in your efforts.

In essence, the Action Plan component of the Bold Life Formula acknowledges that pursuing an intentional change in your life that adds meaning and value is not necessarily an easy task.

However, by applying proven scientific methodologies, various Action Plan steps can be employed that dramatically increase the chance for success.

In the latter sections of this book, these Action Plan steps will be discussed further while providing additional resources to help you create a plan specific for your pursuits. In doing so, you will be well prepared to not only embark on positive and intentional change, but also persist in these efforts throughout your life.

By utilizing the Bold Life Formula, you can choose to become the best you can be.

The Formula is simple and straightforward, and all it takes is for you to want to invite intentional change into your life to realize your greatest potential.

Anyone can lead a Bold Life, no matter where they are. All it requires is a desire and commitment to stretch yourself toward the pursuit of true excellence. Are you ready to take that challenge and make your life a bold one? If so, let your journey begin!

MAX

BOLD LIFE FORMULA WORKSHEET

My Pillar: ACHIEVEMENT
My Goal: TO MAKE A BETTER LIFE FOR MYSELF

In chapter IV of Edward A. Steiner's "On the Trail of The Immigrant," some of the challenges and stresses that faced immigrants entering through Ellis Island are documented.[18] Steiner posed the adroit question, "Will they let me in? It is a serious matter to many a man who has invested his all in

---

[18] Edward A. Steiner, *On the Trail of the Immigrant* (Revell, 1900)

a ticket for the New World to face the possibility of rejection."

Max arrived at Ellis Island in New York City on July 20ᵗʰ, 1906. He had turned 17 since he left his parents. Stress was high. You would think that after enduring such travel hardship, the arrival in the U.S. would be celebratory. But a "mission accomplished" moment it was not. Max had many new challenges ahead.

Steiner wrote, "Let no one believe that landing on the shores of 'The land of the free, and the home of the brave' is a pleasant experience; it is a hard, harsh fact, surrounded by the grinding machinery of the law, which sifts, picks, and chooses; admitting the fit and excluding the weak and helpless."

Exhausted from travel, malnourished and unwashed, Max now had to navigate the tricky labyrinth of customs processing on Ellis Island. Danger was everywhere. If unable to maneuver, the consequences were severe: deportation in steerage again in even harsher conditions. The cruise line was required to take the unacceptable back for free... and they barely provided for those passengers.

After being examined, questioned, solicited for bribes and threatened with deportation, Max finally got through Ellis Island. When he walked the streets of Manhattan for the first time, Max had 33 cents in his pocket.

The city was overwhelming. There was a lot for him to learn and accomplish. He could not speak or read English and his formal education was minimal. He needed to find work, a place to sleep and a community to help him through his new country, the New World.

His first job was as a busboy where he made a few cents, ate leftover food and, after closing, slept in the restaurant with a tablecloth as his blanket. He would later make his living washing windows in NYC. Being a small, light of weight man, Max would be held by rope from rooftops and use his shammy and water pail to clean the soot off of windows.

Over the next six years, Max worked and saved his money, and migrated to Montville, Connecticut. His goal to have his own farm and a family was finally at hand.

Max's first child was born in 1912. He had eight children and lived on his farm until he passed in June of 1970 at the age of 83.

Chapter 9 – Creating Your Bold Life Action Plan

"Give me six hours to chop down a tree and I'll spend the first four sharpening the axe." - unknown

In the prior chapters, we discussed the major components of the Bold Life equation. The first component of the equation involves an assessment of each of the Seven Pillars, while the second component demands setting Bold Goals. However, while assessing the Seven Pillars and determining your Bold Goals are critical steps in the process of attaining a Bold Life, neither will allow you to achieve one without the third and final component of the equation: an Action Plan.

All too often, we get bogged down in the planning stages when it comes to pursuing our goals. Likewise, we can spend too much energy on analyzing the steps we should take or in organizing resources that we think we might need. These are valued steps in achieving goals, but they must eventually be coupled with action in order to see results. After all, we are generally not rewarded for a great idea unless it is implemented and actually bears fruit.

With this in mind, this chapter is dedicated to helping you appreciate the importance of an Action Plan, as well as putting that plan into action. In order to achieve a Bold Life, you must not only define your Bold Goals and their meaning to you personally, but you must also invest energy and effort in their pursuit. In doing so, many additional rewards will be realized that you may otherwise fail to appreciate.

Don't Get Lost in Seesaw Park

Hopefully, the previous chapters have convinced you of the importance of finding your inspiration within the Seven Pillars. Did it work? Are you convinced?

Good. Now put that stuff out of your mind, because if you dwell too much on the considerations of which Pillars contain your Bold Goals and which of those Pillars demand your immediate attention, you can become lost... lost in Seesaw Park.

Imagine a park full of seesaws—yes, seesaws, those playground staples that have kids sitting on either end of a balanced plank, bouncing up and down.

Now picture Pillars resting on the ends of those planks. These Pillars represent your potential Bold Goals, like a fruitful career as an investment banker or running a marathon or two. Or they could be goals like paying off all your debts or traveling the world.

More often than not, these potential Bold Goals are at odds with each other. For instance, the hours required for a career in investment banking don't exactly jibe with the hours required to train for a marathon, and how on Earth could you travel around Earth without incurring at least some debt?

Welcome to Seesaw Park, where choosing between these Pillars (that are bobbing up and down) can leave you stuck in indecision!

The previously discussed Worksheets—the Pillar Ranker, Pillar Planner, and Goal Refiner—can all help you avoid Seesaw Park, at least on a conceptual level. But the best weapon you have against the potentially perilous paralysis of choice is…

…The Action Plan. The Action Plan, if done correctly, will lay out all the steps required to reach your Bold Goal. In fact, if done correctly, the Action Plan will lay out contingencies for if (or maybe an inevitable "when") you fall off the horse. It will even make sure you have a support team in place to help with encouragement when you need it.

Ultimately, a good Action Plan will help you avoid Seesaw Park and continue on to your Bold Goals.

The Building Blocks to an Action Plan

Planning is key to success. It almost goes without saying that the more prepared you are, the more likely you will succeed.

Unfortunately, many people become frightened by the idea of building a plan. Maybe they're intimidated by what they view as too complex, or maybe they're put off by the possibility of a misstep in the planning stage, causing the whole endeavor to go awry.

But there is nothing to fear!

The easiest way is to start with the big picture first, then build more detail as your thinking develops. Imagine your Action Plan as a series of blocks—blocks that are gradually stacked into a set of stairs.

This is the concept behind the Building Block Plan Worksheet, which is a big picture vision of the steps taken to reach your Bold Goal.

A Building Block Plan is something like a conceptual house plan. If you wanted an architect to design you a house, you'd first sketch out a general idea of what you wanted—a bedroom here, a living room there. But that sketch isn't actionable. No carpenter could take that sketch and build a house from it (or at least, not a house that would be structurally sound!).

Instead, the architect would use your sketch to draw more detailed plans, plans that would, at some point, lay out intricate electrical and plumbing schematics, etcetera.

(It's also worth noting that sometimes those detailed architectural plans are tweaked and revised while they're being executed, depending on how construction is going. This is very much true of Action Plans, too. They can evolve into different plans over time – and that's okay!)

The Building Block Plan is that sketch of your dream house. It's not a granular breakdown of the day-to-day tasks and benchmarks needed to accomplish your Bold Goals (there are other Worksheets for that). It's your strategic plan painted in broad brushstrokes.

Consider Justin and Kaisorn McCurry, and their Bold Goal of retiring at 33-years old.

The broader steps of their Action Plan's building blocks would be to cut down on their expenses, save up money, and invest wisely.

But of course, there were multiple steps in between those – steps that broke down the day-to-day and month-to-month tasks that needed to be done to accomplish the bigger steps of cutting down expenses, saving money and investing wisely. Maybe those steps would include things like cutting their subscription to cable TV, or starting a coin jar or piggy bank, or buying some long-term bonds or other debt instruments.

Only when all those steps were done together, and each of the smaller goals that made up the building blocks was achieved, could the McCurry's Bold Goal be reached.

Now consider the Building Block Plan Worksheet.

Think of your ultimate Bold Goal. Have you got that image in your mind? Good. Now imagine three to five steps it would take to reach that Bold Goal.

Write each of those three to five steps at the top of the columns, each step commanding its own column.

Once you've completed that, you can use the lines below each step to break down the smaller, granular things that need to be accomplished to complete those bigger steps.

BUILDING BLOCK PLAN WORKSHEET

▶ There will be multiple steps taken to accomplish your Bold Goal. At the top of each column, write down each of those steps. Below those steps, write down the tasks that must be completed to move on to the next step. This is your Action Plan, broken down into broader brushstrokes (at the top of the columns) and more granular details within each column.

My Bold Goal is: _____

$BL = B + BG + AP$

How does it look filled out? Good? Inspiring? Congrats, this is the beginning of your Action Plan.

There are a few other facets that need to be addressed before the Action Pan is complete, though.

For instance, what happens if, while galloping toward your Bold Goal, you fall off the horse?

The Fall Off the Horse Plan

A multitude of eventualities and opportunities for even the best-laid plans to go awry all point to one simple fact: falling off the horse while galloping determinedly towards your Bold Goal is almost inevitable.

A sprained ankle while training for that marathon? Certainly bad. Discouraging, even.

Struggling with studying for your Series 7 while trundling toward that future as an investment banker? It happens.

But while it's hard (impossible, actually) to plan and prepare for every little thing that could go wrong or get in your way, it is possible to lay down some contingencies for the things you think could likely cause problems.

Welcome to the Fall Off the Horse Plan.

The concept behind the Fall Off the Horse Plan Worksheet is simple: list the ways something could go wrong as you strive to reach your Bold Goal, and beside each of those falls, list two remedies.

MY FALL OFF
THE HORSE PLANS

Type of Fall	Two ways to get back on
1. _____	☐ _____ ☐ _____
2. _____	☐ _____ ☐ _____
3. _____	☐ _____ ☐ _____
4. _____	☐ _____ ☐ _____

Sometimes a fall off the horse while galloping toward your Bold Goal is inevitable. How will you react? The best reaction is to be proactive - meaning, figure out what will likely make you fall, then determine how best to get back in the saddle.

PBL = M + SG + AP

Remember: it is far better to be proactive than reactive. In other words, tackling these potential problems before they arise is a better option than struggling to find solutions when you've fallen out of the saddle and you're face-down in the mud.

It's also worth noting that the ways you can get back in the saddle can involve help from others or help from no one but yourself. However, if you need help from others, there's a Worksheet for that…

The Bold Commitment and Support Team

A Bold Goal isn't something you should keep secret. In fact, the simple act of announcing your Bold Goal to others is a form of commitment – by publicly stating, "I'm going to do this," you are making a firm resolution to accomplish something and bringing others into the resolution.

After all, if you set a goal and tell no one of that goal, then fail to reach that goal, you're accountable to only yourself. But if you bring others into it, you're now accountable to them as well.

The top half of the Bold Commitment and Support Team Worksheet deals with those with whom you'd make your intentions known to, and they can be your significant other, friends, peers… anyone, really.

The second half of the Worksheet is for listing your support team, i.e., those who will help you in case you fall off the horse while en route towards your Bold Goal. They, too, might be your significant other, friends or peers.

MY BOLD COMMITMENT
& SUPPORT TEAM

People I have made my Commitment public to (at least 2)   Date Completed

☐ _____   _____

☐ _____   _____

☐ _____   _____

People who will help me when I Fall Off the Horse   Date Asked

☐ _____   _____

☐ _____   _____

☐ _____   _____

PBL = PI + SPG + AP

What sort of help would they offer? That can vary, but more often than not, it might be a kind word or encouragement… or a swift kick in the pants!

Vivica A. Fox is a very accomplished lady, but it wasn't always that way for her and her story is inspiring for anyone who seeks greatness at any level. She has incorporated important elements of the Bold Life Formula into her life and they have served her well.

I was fortunate to be introduced to Vivica by Pam McElvane, CEO of Diversity MBA Magazine (DMBA), just after Vivica had completed her keynote speech at DMBA's September 2018 Annual Conference in Chicago, IL. She had spoken for 50 minutes and participated in an almost 40-minute question-and-answer session led by Pam. Vivica's message, built around her book "Every Day I'm Hustling," had excited the crowd. For those of you who have not given speeches followed by Q's and A's, the time on stage is exciting yet exhausting. Pam runs a tight ship as I had been on a panel just before Vivica for almost 80 minutes. When Vivica walked off the stage, her energy level was still amazingly high. I would learn more about that energy when I interviewed her about 90 minutes later.

Vivica grew up in Indianapolis, Indiana, where she was one of four children born to William and Everlyena Fox. It was a sports-oriented family, and Vivica learned about competition and getting back up from sporting activities from them. After getting knocked down by her brother in a basketball game, she was pretty distraught. Her father smartly told her, "Angie, if you want to hang with the big boys, you're gonna get knocked down. It's on you to get up."[19] It was a lesson Vivica would never forget.

Part of Vivica's keynote in Chicago was about how a 53-year-old black woman in Hollywood could take her career to new levels of success – a

---

[19] Vivica Fox, "Every Day I'm Hustling" St. Martin's Press 2019.

success that many would say is very difficult considering how youth reigns in her industry. One of Vivica's lessons that day incorporated the fundamental premise of a Bold Life: The notion that you can live a Bold Life <u>at any age.</u>

Her message of always giving your all in pursuit of your dreams is her calling card. Every day she is hustling! That day in September showed that she means it.

Vivica's commitment to hustle and her Bold Goal started when her mother gave her a loan and some very important advice during a very hard time in her life. Vivica had called her mother and was looking for advice on what to do to get her career on track.

> *"Write a letter," Mom told me. "Put it in your Bible and pray about it. He will bring it back to you."*
>
> *So, I got on my knees. And I wrote this:*
>
> *"I want to be successful. I want to be a star and I want to work as an actress. And I've got a taste of things, but it seems I can't get over the hump. It seems I'm always almost just making it and then coming up a little bit short. If you could just help me to stay focused and help me to stay positive, I promise that I'll be good. And do good. And give back."[20]*

---

[20] Fox, Vivica A. "Every Day I'm Hustling" (p. xi). St. Martin's Press. Kindle Edition.

Without realizing it, Vivica had written her goal and built her Commitment Team.

Building your Commitment Team is an important part of the Action Plan, so the Commitment and Support Team Worksheet is an important one to fill out. It is just not an exercise for you to do. There is a reason why we also ask that you give your completed Bold Life Goal to your Commitment Team in writing: it increases your chances of success!

*Don't just take my word for it that building a commitment team works. The world's largest professional membership organization, the Association for Talent Development (ATD) did an accountability study in 2017. ATD supports those who develop the knowledge and skills of employees, improves performance, and helps to achieve results for the organizations they serve since 1943. They are experts in performance methods. The study showed that **people increase their chances of succeeding with goals by 65% if they make a commitment to someone. The chances of success increase by 95% if the person also makes a specific accountability appointment!** Wow! Making a commitment to someone really makes a difference!*

Bold Goals can sometimes be long shots. We, therefore, need every improved chance we can get. In the case of Vivica, the chances of becoming a star were low, but she increased her odds significantly that day. Her mother gave her some very wise advice.

Write your goal and make a commitment. Vivica's commitment team was a strong one: her mother and the Lord!

Another of Vivica's key messages that day was about surrounding yourself with supportive people – your Fall Off the Horse Team.

Vivica, in her speech, discussed how her support team had helped her throughout her career, particularly as she has aged to a wildly great older actress. She embraces her age and has a motto for it: "Don't get older, get f***ing better."

In her book, Vivica devotes a full chapter to this important concept. The chapter is titled "Get Your Squad Together - You'll Need Them."

Everyone on their Bold journey will face challenges and need help at times along the way. It is never an easy path up the Bold Mountain. Vivica's message is to build a great team of supporters. She said, "If I'm really preaching anything with this book, it's that positivity works. Surround yourself with good people who want you to succeed, and once you do, give back and help the next generation along."[21]

So, my time with Vivica was finally here. She had just completed over 2 1/2 hours of speeches,

---

[21] Fox, Vivica A. "Every Day I'm Hustling" (p. xi). St. Martin's Press. Kindle Edition.

questions, book signings and pictures. I looked at her and asked, "Vivica are you sure you want to sit with me now for an interview in front of the cameras?" I knew she was likely exhausted and wanted to offer her an out or a break.

She looked me in the eye and said, "Ed, of course I am ready. Let's do it!" She had just made me feel like the most important person in the room and she proved again that every day she is hustling! Her energy and passion are inspiring.

Our interview was special. She was very gracious with her time and her answers. Her video interview and story I wrote from that day can be found on the Bold Business site.[22] There is a link there to buy her book on Amazon.

My last question that day led to a fantastic answer.

I asked, "What last bit of advice do you have to share?"

Her answer, "You only have one life to live, live it bold."

I hope her story inspires you to do so.

The Yearly-, Monthly-, and Daily Implementation Plans

You've used the Pillars to find the inspiration for your Bold Goal. You've applied the concept of SMART to

---

[22] https://www.boldbusiness.com/human-achievement/vivica-a-fox-gold-tips-from-every-day-im-hustling/

make sure your goal is doable, and you've weighed the pros and cons. You've laid out the building blocks, notified your Commitment Team and Support Team. What's next?

Well, now is when you get a bit more granular with your planning and start figuring out what needs to be done on a yearly basis, monthly basis and daily basis.

Yes, there are Worksheets for this, but when you tackle them, keep in mind that you've already ironed out a strategic plan. There is no need to use the same broad brushstrokes you used on the Building Block Plan. When figuring out the yearly, monthly and daily stuff, it's okay— necessary, even—to go a little finer with the details.

Consider the Yearly Implementation Plan.

MY BOLD GOALS
YEARLY PLAN

▶ What tasks do you need to accomplish on a yearly basis to reach your Bold Goals? What tasks do you need to accomplish yearly that have nothing to do with your Bold Goals? Use this worksheet to layout both kinds of tasks. Once that's done, you will get a better sense of the things on that might be distracting you. You will at least get a better handle on things that are keeping you from your goal!

Yearly Tasks for Accomplishing Bold Goal

1. _____
2. _____
3. _____
4. _____
5. _____

Yearly Tasks Unrelated to Accomplishing Bold Goal

1. _____
2. _____
3. _____
4. _____
5. _____

$PBL = PI + SPG + (AP)$

Presumably, your Bold Goal is so bold it will take more than a year or two to complete. Therefore, there will be tasks that need to be completed or benchmarks to meet, over the course of a few years. Put them down— as well as other things not directly related to your Bold Goal (but which can affect your progress)—on this sheet.

For example, if your Bold Goal is to retire at 33 like the McCurry Family, your yearly tasks might be to gradually reduce food spending until it reaches a certain point at the 12-month mark.

Or, if your Bold Goal is to set a record running a marathon, your yearly tasks might include particular paces and times, or runs completed.

Have career goals? Then your yearly tasks could range from leadership courses or certifications completed to annual performance review scores… you get the point.

Ultimately, the Yearly-, Monthly- and Daily Implementation Plans are meant to simply help you implement your grander Action Plan, so when you fill them out, keep that in mind. They are important… but when it comes to realizing your Bold Goal, the Building Block Plan, and the Commitment Team and Support Team Worksheets are where the true battle is won or lost.

Below is the Monthly Implementation Plan Worksheet, which is to be filled out in a similar fashion to the Yearly Implementation Plan Worksheet (except on a month-to-month level).

In the appendices of this book, you can find the Daily Implementation Plan Worksheet (as well as all the other Worksheets, of course).

MY BOLD GOALS
MONTHLY PLAN

▶ What tasks do you need to accomplish on a monthly basis to reach your Bold Goals? What tasks do you need to accomplish monthly that have nothing to do with your Bold Goals? Use this worksheet to layout both kinds of tasks. Once that's done, you will get a better sense of the things on that might be distracting you. You will at least get a better handle on things that are keeping you from your goal!

Monthly Tasks for Accomplishing Bold Goal

1. _____
2. _____
3. _____
4. _____
5. _____

Monthly Tasks Unrelated to Accomplishing Bold Goal

1. _____
2. _____
3. _____
4. _____
5. _____

$PBL = M + S^2G + Ap$

The Bold Life Formula Worksheet – The Final Step!

You've done Worksheets galore and have your future—at least in regard to your Bold Goal—plotted out. Congrats! You're almost there!

The last piece of the puzzle ties everything together and puts your Action Plan and all the pertinent information in one place. Behold, the Bold Life Formula Worksheet!

BOLD LIFE FORMULA WORKSHEET

▶ Who will help you if you fall off the horse en route to your Bold Goal? Who is part of your Bold Support Team? Give a signed Bold Life Formula Worksheet to at least two members of your Support Team, and list who they are and when you gave them the sheets. Below that, list anyone else who might help you - via encouragement, motivation, or whatever.

My Goal: ....

My Pillar: _____

Is it Smart?   Yes ☐   No ☐
Is it Stretch?   Yes ☐   No ☐

Why is this Pillar inspirational to me?

_____

_____

_____

Do I have my Fall Off The Horse Plan?   Yes ☐   No ☐
Do I have my Support Team?   Yes ☐   No ☐

My Action Plan

                                                                GOAL

                                                    STEP 5

                                        STEP 4

                            STEP 3

                STEP 2

    STEP 1

I hereby affirm that my Action Plan is laid out,
my commitment is made public, and I have a Support Team

$PBL = Pi + SG + AP$

As you can see, if you've done all the previous Worksheets leading up to this one, you already have the information – your goal, your Pillar, your building block steps for your Action Plan, etc.

However, there is one important distinction. Note the oath requiring your signature. Much like the promise made to your Commitment Team, this, too, is a promise. A promise to yourself!

Ideally, you will fill out copies of the Bold Life Formula Worksheet, sign them, and give one to each member of your Commitment Team.

(Although if, like Vivica Fox, you make your commitment to God, sticking to the Bold Life Formula Worksheet will do just fine.)

Okay, now that all the paperwork is done, you're almost ready to attack that Bold Goal. What's next?

Time to choose to act and choose to succeed.

JUSTIN AND KAISORN MCCURRY

BOLD LIFE FORMULA WORKSHEET

My Pillar: FINANCES

My Goal: TO RETIRE AT 33

Justin and Kaisorn McCurry managed to rein in their expenses, save, and invest so they could retire at 33. How did they do it?

They, of course, had an Action Plan, which was born from a Building Block Plan.

BUILDING BLOCK PLAN WORKSHEET

▶ There will be multiple steps taken to accomplish your Bold Goal. At the top of each column, write down each of those steps. Below those steps, write down the tasks that must be completed to move on to the next step. This is your Action Plan, broken down into broader brushstrokes (at the top of the columns) and more granular details within each column.

My Bold Goal is: __TO RETIRE AT 33__

CUTDOWN ON EXPENSES	SAVE UP MONEY	INVEST WISELY		
CUTOFF CABLE TV	PUT MOST OF PAYCHECK INTO SAVINGS	RESEARCH STOCKS		
BUY USED CAR		START PORTFOLIO		
EAT AT HOME, NOT RESTAURANTS				

FSL = Fi + S/G + Ap

But another vital piece of the puzzle they had was a weighing of the pros and cons that resulted in a complete buy-in by not just Justin, but his family as well. After all, how successful could the McCurry's truly be if only Justin were to live frugally?

JUSTIN AND KAISORN MCCURRY

BOLD GOALS
PROS VS. CONS

▶The execution of any Bold Goal will have an upside and a downside, both as they affect you and affect the world around you. Use this Pro vs. Con sheet to determine the cost/benefit analysis of your potential Bold undertaking.

My Bold Goal is _TO RETIRE AT 33_

Self Pros	Self Cons
1. WILL HAVE MORE TIME TO ENJOY LIFE WITHOUT WORKING	1. FRUGAL LIVING MEANS NO EXTRAVAGANT VACATIONS
2.	2. NO EXPENSIVE CLOTHES
3.	3.
4.	4.

External Pros	External Cons
1. FAMILY WILL BE ABLE TO SPEND MORE TIME TOGETHER	1. FRUGAL LIVING MEANS LESS EATING IN RESTAURANTS
2.	2. NO CABLE TV!
3.	3.
4.	4.

PBL = Pi + SPG + Ap

The pros and cons of the commitment to your goal must be fully considered. Norcross calls this step 2 of the five steps to change, Prep: Planning before Leaping. If Justin's wife was not on board with their goal and committed to the plan, it would have likely failed. His wife needed to buy-in to frugal living, high savings and low cost investing. A plan like this could be difficult for many couples.

Here is what Justin writes on his _Root of Good_ blog:

"Optimal Spouse Selection

[My wife] and I married right before I finished law school... Our similar outlooks on personal finances have been a huge wealth generator.

It may come as no surprise that we are both very frugal about virtually everything. We agree on saving a large part of our incomes. We take vacations offseason because crowds are thinner and our wallets get fatter (er, less thin). Our furniture might be uncharitably described as dorm room chic. Our kids wear hand me downs alongside inexpensively purchased new clothes. We live in a modest neighborhood and drive modest cars.

We made these frugal choices so that one day we can retire early and not have the stress and time demands from a regular job burdening our daily lives. There is more to life."

Although my Project Bold Life research shows discouraging numbers for many people in the Pillar of Financial Bold Goals. The McCurry's story and the FIRE movement are inspiring looks at how everyday people can accomplish financial independence and very Bold Goals.

Chapter 10 – Choosing to Act, Choosing to Succeed

"By failing to prepare, you're preparing to fail." -
Benjamin Franklin

In an effort to achieve the Bold Life you desire, it is important to adopt an Action Plan that leads you in the right direction. But even prior to implementing an Action Plan, you need to adopt an action mentality to facilitate your success.

What is an action mentality? In short, it's a mindset that appreciates the importance of action in achieving important goals, and it also acknowledges the common barriers that may stand in the way. By embracing an action mentality, a tendency for inertia and inaction can be overcome so that Bold Life Goals will be better realized.

TAKING ACTION REQUIRES AN ACTION MENTALITY

PROJECT BOLD LIFE

Unfortunately, a failure to act on well-developed plans is quite common. We might appreciate the Seven

Pillars that are important to our life, and we may identify key Bold Goals that we need to pursue. But as we stand on the threshold of putting a plan into action, we falter.

Some of us get stuck in the planning and thinking stages and never take the next step. Others are paralyzed by fear that prevents them from taking action.

As a result, goals are never attained, and the Bold Life of which they dream never materializes.

In considering this, it is important to appreciate various fears that may interfere with us taking action and implementing our plan to attain our Bold Goals.

By far, the most common fear is a fear of failure. Because we are choosing to explore new and unknown territory in our life, we become anxious about what might occur. If we fail, we fear that our self-confidence will waiver and that others will judge us for our faults.

So, rather than moving forward and taking action, we stand at the edge paralyzed by our fear. As a result, nothing is accomplished.

Don't be paralyzed by fear!

(Note: this paralysis isn't quite the same as the paralysis brought about by the indecision found in Seesaw Park… but the end result is the same. In both instances, you are hesitating to act when action is what you really need to be doing.)

One of the most important aspects of adopting an action mentality is to shift the way you perceive failure. Certainly, Action Plans would be much easier if we always succeeded at everything we tried. But in reality, this would rob us of many wonderful opportunities to learn and grow. Indeed, Bold Goals are the target achievements for our efforts, but much is gained during the journey in attaining these goals. Specifically, the failures we encounter along the way, and the lessons learned from them, are immensely valuable in our Bold Life pursuits. Thus, it is very important that we appreciate this fact to help us adopt an action mentality.

In addition to the fear of failure, achieving success is another common fear that can hinder an action mindset. Remarkably, some people fear attaining the very goals they desire because such success also represents an unknown situation. Such fears may be driven by stories of others who have achieved success and struggled with its new lifestyle. Others simply fear the unknown because it represents a change that takes them out of their current comfort zone. Understanding this, it is important to appreciate what it means to pursue a Bold Life. In addition to the bold nature of the goals you choose, embarking on any major change is considered quite bold as well.

Given this, it is essential that you acknowledge your specific concerns about your potential success and address them one by one. By doing so, you will reduce their capacity to hold you back and again facilitate an action mindset in the process.

Acknowledge the Benefits of Taking Action

In addition to overcoming inherent inertia and specific fears in adopting an action mentality, it is also helpful to appreciate the advantages that taking action provides. As noted, when we choose to act and pursue our goals, we invite the opportunity for feedback to occur.

Failure is one type of feedback that might occur, which should be seen as an opportunity rather than a setback. In essence, failure provides important information that we can use to further refine our efforts going forward. Thus, taking action naturally provides us with additional insights that can help us progress and excel.

Taking action helps in other ways, as well. One benefit of taking action that is often underappreciated relates to the growth of new resources that occur when we energize an Action Plan. By taking action, tangible proof that we are moving in a specific direction can be readily seen. As a result, others will notice and offer advice as well as support that may not have previously existed.

Likewise, our actions, through our failures or from the assistance of others, can highlight additional resources we may need or can use to better achieve our goals. While inaction may keep these potentially valuable resources in the dark, action brings them to the forefront for us to better appreciate them.

Understanding the benefits that additional resources and feedback provide when we take action promotes an ongoing action mentality. But taking those first steps encourages us in other ways, too.

With each progressive step in the right direction, we increasingly commit ourselves to pursue our goals. And as greater investments are made, there is a progressively lower chance that we will get stuck along the way. This phenomenon has been well-recognized and termed an "escalation of commitment," which encourages us to keep moving forward. Because we naturally want to gain the greatest return on the actions we have already taken, we are motivated to persist in our efforts to attain our goals.

While past investments and actions serve as a motivation to keep the ball rolling, action also helps us foster better habits as well. As many have realized, taking that first step can be the most difficult. However, with each successive step, not only do things become easier, but we also begin to develop positive habits that support the Action Plan we are implementing. Thus, rather than becoming stuck in inaction, we acquire a healthy appetite and constructive practices for action and progress. All of these outcomes that result from our initials actions serve to perpetuate forward momentum in our pursuit of a Bold Life.

Finally, the decision to take those first steps and begin our Bold Life plan also puts forth a very positive message. By choosing to act, we tell others around us that we expect our actions to produce results. Besides encouraging feedback and additional resources, it also creates an aura of positivity around our efforts. When we choose to act, we invite the law of positive attraction to help us advance further toward our goals. This law of attraction can manifest itself in a variety of ways, but in every instance, it serves to pave the way for ongoing successes.

Thus, by choosing to act, we create an environment in which the pursuit of our Bold Goals can thrive.

The Paradox of Bold Life Goals

As has been discussed earlier, Bold Goals are those that stretch you to be the best you can be. In many instances, these types of goals allow you to make a tremendous impact on the lives of others as well as society at large. Because of this, such Bold Goals can be rather intimidating. Analyzing, planning and organizing an Action Plan for these types of goals can quickly consume your thoughts, making it increasingly difficult to develop a cohesive strategy for success. In essence, the magnitude of the Bold Goal itself can actually cause you to be prone to inaction.

This is the "paradox" of Bold Goals. While our intentions in defining and attaining Bold Goals are to become the best we can be, sometimes these same goals can intimidate us and cause us to become paralyzed. Given the enormity and/or degree of importance of such goals, we become overwhelmed and fail to act. Likewise, these same goals may be so encompassing that we don't know where to start or how to arrive at the final destination. Thus, despite our best intentions, we end up no better than we were at the beginning.

Fortunately, there is an effective approach to Bold Goals that enables us to be less intimidated and more successful in our pursuits. Rather than focusing on the overarching Bold Goal itself, you instead create a series of smaller goals that can lead you in that direction. This strategy provides a more reasonable and manageable plan that is less overwhelming, and it offers you the opportunity to pursue your Bold Goal in smaller steps that are easier to grasp. By focusing your attention on smaller steps along the way, you will be less likely to get distracted and more likely to persevere in your ongoing efforts.

In considering this, it is important to keep smaller steps in mind when creating your Action Plan in the pursuit of your Bold Goals. Rather than trying to determine how to get from A to B, develop a roadmap that includes a number of different steps and "mini-goals" that will ultimately help you arrive at your destination.

You will likely define a number of smaller achievements that you will need to accomplish that will enable you to eventually attain the Bold Goal being considered. Once these have been identified, you can then set out to achieve these with less stress and anxiety.

By identifying and pursuing smaller and more "digestible" targets, you will be less likely to feel overwhelmed and more likely to jump into action.

It is worth noting that the smaller steps that you identify may very well not be sequential in nature. For example, the first mini-goal you pursue might not be a foundational achievement needed for success. Instead, it might be a task that makes achieving another foundational achievement more likely. Likewise, pursuing several different mini-goals at once may make the most sense in some situations. Thus, the purpose of creating mini-goals is not necessarily to create a linear path toward achieving your Bold Goals. Instead, it is simply a strategy to empower you to take action and move forward by creating several tasks that are easier to attain.

Overall, the smaller steps and mini-goals you identify will culminate in your ability to successfully achieve your Bold Goals. Through this approach, you will be less likely to get discouraged, and you will be able to receive more frequent and positive feedback along the way.

Likewise, by celebrating the attainment of each mini-goal, you allow yourself to be empowered in your overall goal pursuits. Thus, rather than being intimidated and overwhelmed, you become energized and excited to continue moving ahead. In doing so, you eliminate the possibility that the paradox of Bold Goals might interfere with your efforts to attain a truly Bold Life.

Personal Characteristics for an Effective Action Plan

When it comes to the Action Plan you lay out to achieve your Bold Goals, adopting an action mindset and a mini-goal strategy are important approaches. But at the same time, there are specific personal characteristics that you should cultivate to facilitate your success as well. These attributes will make it more likely that you will sustain progress along the way and ultimately achieve the Bold Goals you have defined. These personal characteristics include resilience, self-motivation, and a committed focus.

Resilience can be defined as the psychological strength to persevere in your pursuits and to manage the challenges along the way. By having the mental resolve and strength to pursue your Bold Goals, you will be better able to implement your Action Plan efficiently and successfully. Resiliency allows you to best utilize your skills and talents to solve problems while developing innovative ways to improve results. And even when first (and perhaps second and third) attempts fail, you will have the fortitude to persevere.

With this in mind, it is important to consider how to enhance your resiliency. Several strategies can be utilized, and one of the most powerful is social support.

Individuals with social support naturally have increased resilience because they have the resources to lean on when needed. In addition, maintaining a positive perspective with confidence that your efforts can evoke an anticipated change also enhances resilience. And lastly, exhibiting emotional control when challenges arise allows you to stay calm and focused in completing various tasks. Each of these can improve your level of resilience and increase your chances of success.

The second important characteristic that improves your chances for Action Plan success is self-motivation. Self-motivation refers to the personal drive to attain whatever goals you set out to accomplish. In order to foster strong self-confidence, it helps to have a growth mindset, which describes the inherent belief in your own self-abilities. This not only includes a belief that you can learn from enhanced knowledge and experiences but also implies you believe you can overcome obstacles while taking advantage of opportunities.

In order to enhance your self-confidence, seek personal inspirations to encourage your efforts and beliefs. Likewise, positive affirmations and encouraging thoughts can also foster greater self-confidence. Through these practices, you will further your abilities to effectively implement your Action Plan.

The final characteristic that enhances Action Plan success is the ability to maintain a strong sense of focus. The ability to maintain focus implies that you can direct your attention selectively on those items that are high priority. This naturally requires a capacity to block out other distractions and so-called "noise" that might interfere with your ultimate success. It also assumes an ability to remain calm and strong when faced with difficulties and stress. Through mental practices that might include meditation and enhanced awareness exercises, a greater capacity for focused attention can evolve. As a result, this will provide you with the ability to act more purposefully and with greater efficiency as you pursue your Bold Goals.

Developing and maintaining these three important personal characteristics means you will have much greater success with your Bold Goal. These attributes, combined with an action mentality and strategies that avoid the Bold Goal paradox, provide you with the key elements needed for implementing your Bold Life Action Plan.

By utilizing the strategies and tools in this chapter with that Action Plan, you can successfully attain the Bold Life that you deserve.

Section 11: Living Bold: Finding Your Passion, Goals and Success

Chapter 11 – The Most Rewarding Pillar: Health

"Health is a state of complete harmony of the body, mind, and spirit. When one is free from physical disabilities and mental distractions, the gates of the soul open." - B.K.S. Iyengar

As life goes on, investing in our health becomes an activity we may neglect or take for granted. But no different than a career or a retirement plan, making regular and consistent investments in our health is necessary in order for us to achieve our full potential. Sadly, for many, it's only after a "wake-up call" that we suddenly realize the value and importance of health as a central Pillar in our own personal success. Fortunately, choosing to boldly invest in health is something each of us can do regardless of our current state of affairs. Everyone has the power to make tremendous changes in their lives when they commit to bold health goals.

The pursuit of good health is an important strategy when seeking to live the boldest life possible. As a foundation, good health enables us to thrive and be fully engaged with everything and everyone around us. At the same time, good health allows us to better fulfill our goals and explore our passions. And good health allows for powerful insights about ourselves that can help us in times of adversity.

For all of these reasons, health represents one of the most rewarding of the Seven Pillars.

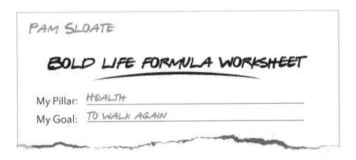

PAM SLOATE

BOLD LIFE FORMULA WORKSHEET

My Pillar: HEALTH
My Goal: TO WALK AGAIN

I introduced you to Pam Sloate in Chapter 2. She is an amazing role model for people who don't let challenges get in the way. "The Little Engine That Tried" aptly describes her. Her story touches a few pillars.

Pam is a very accomplished woman. She grew up in Scarsdale, New York, and worked hard as a youth. She was admitted to an Ivy League school, Brown University, in 1982. She did well at Brown and after Brown earned her law degree from New York University, one of the top law schools in the country. Yet all her schooling did not prepare Pam for the Bold Life she would lead.

Pam inherited a rare disease called dystonia, which is a neurological movement disorder. Specifically, her diagnosis was early-onset torsion dystonia, also known as Oppenheim's dystonia. With this condition, sustained muscle contractions cause twisting and repetitive movements and/or abnormal fixed postures.

In her blog, Dystonia Muse, Pam described it in her own words:[23]

> I have D-Y-S-T-O-N-I-A? No, it's not a former Soviet Socialist Republic but a neurological movement disorder.
>
> So what is Dystonia? Let's set aside medical formalities and fast-forward to practical realities. Imagine you're trying to jot down a grocery list and, quite inconveniently, someone jerks your elbow up and down, making it difficult – if not impossible – to control your writing.
>
> Or maybe you tackle something complicated like walking across a room. You lift your leg to begin that first step when a mischievous troll screws up your balance by pulling your foot inward, causing you to land on the side of your foot and desperately search for stability. Simultaneously, some imp twists your knee while your hip dips and swings in a motion that would swirl a hula-hoop.

Over time Dystonia can be extremely debilitating. Pam was first diagnosed at 8 ½ years old. She

---

[23] https://dystoniamuse.com/

initially did not want to bring attention to her challenges and would do her best to hide them from people she met. She told me that when she was younger, most disabled people felt their disabilities were something to be ashamed of. People were not as accepting as today and were treated differently. Pam did not want to be treated differently. Her best friends and family knew about the disease and helped her live as normal a life as possible. Pam would not be able to keep her condition low key for long, though. At Brown and at NYU, Pam would pull her typewriter with her to class, as writing and taking notes was close to impossible without using a keyboard.

Unfortunately, the disease would progress. As Pam aged, her symptoms became worse and worse. Hiding the symptoms was no longer an option. She needed a walker to get around, and it

*was not easy for her to get around with it. She
also had difficulty with her speech as her jaw, and
facial muscles just simply could not move in the
way needed. Her mind was sharp. Her muscles
were not accommodating.*

*During the progression of her disease, Pam's
inspiration for health, and particularly to find a
way to live with her condition, grew and became
bold.Her passion for getting her health back led
her to establish a Bold Goal.*

*Her Bold Goal: She wanted to walk again without
the aid of a walker.*

*She also had difficulty with her speech as her jaw
and facial muscles just simply could not move in
the way needed. Her mind was sharp. Her
muscles were not accommodating.*

*Her passion led her to explore all types of
treatments and meds. She got involved with
helping build awareness and raise money for the
Cure of Dystonia. Her parents created a research
fund initiative. This led her to learn about a new
treatment that would require brain implants that
would send different signals to her brain and
muscles. Hopefully, improving her muscular
control and abilities would be the result.*

*Because of her active involvement in the cause,
she was able to procure an early trial procedure.
It would be a significant risk, but the upside was
huge. Pam wanted to give it not only a go for
herself but also all the other people who suffered
from Dystonia.*

*When I first met Pam, she was still using her
walker. This was prior to her surgery and rehab*

program. She talked about working on her goal with excitement and passion.

For many people, when inspiration and passion takeover, any goal is achievable. This was the case for Pam. It took Pam months post-surgery to gradually improve. She became more and more able to move her muscles and walk unaided by her walker.

Pam finally progressed to the point where she was ready to let the world know of her progress. At the age of 52, she announced she was hosting a party—a party to celebrate her throwing away her walker. Pam could finally walk unaided! Certainly, a Bold Goal was achieved.

When I spoke with Pam in late June of 2020, she had recently completed two extensive surgeries for sarcoma, an uncommon cancer. She was, as always, amazingly in good cheer.

I could not get over how this woman who had been fighting a lifetime of challenges from dystonia could now end up with another rare health condition! Talk about bad luck? One huge health issue is enough for anyone to experience. I asked her how she was handling this additional challenge.

She said, "You know something, Ed? Nothing surprises me anymore. I think of myself as 'The Little Engine that Tried.' I am just trying all the time."

She went on to share with me how creating her
blog and telling her story was something she
never thought she would do. The reason?
Disabilities were hidden when she grew up.
When you have gone through as much as Pam
has gone through, your perspective seems to
widen. Pam's perspective is a mile wide.
Understanding that her health challenges made
things very challenging, she appreciates
accomplishments just a little more. She has
earned a law degree, learned to walk again
without her walker, supported a foundation, yet
somehow I could tell her greatest
accomplishment was by helping others deal with
their disabilities. She said, "Disability is not
something to be ashamed of. My efforts I believe

have helped change that. The fact that so many people realize that now, makes me happy."[24]

Pam's Bold Life is an inspiration for all.

Today, she continues her work supporting dystonia. She has moved her sights to another Pillar—giving back—and she is active on the Board of the Dystonia Medical Research Foundation.

Well done, Pam!

---

[24] For more on Pam's thoughts about "the Little Engine That Tried" see https://dystoniamuse.com/2013/05/27/the-little-engine-that-tried/

HEALTH

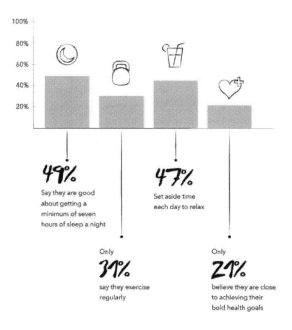

49%

Say they are good about getting a minimum of seven hours of sleep a night

47%

Set aside time each day to relax

Only
31%

say they exercise regularly

Only
21%

believe they are close to achieving their bold health goals

Chapter 12 – The Most Challenging Pillar: Achievement

"To understand the heart and mind of a person, look not at what he has already achieved, but at what he aspires to." - Kahlil Gibran

For many, achievement is simply completing a specific task or goal. But many achievements can leave one feeling empty and unfulfilled.

Bold achievements are those that challenge us, make us better people, and allow us to reach our greatest and boldest potential in life.

As a Pillar of a Bold Life, achievement is highly specific to you as a person. And those goals that are the most challenging are often those that allow you to truly become your absolute best.

Achievement is an inherent part of the human experience, and the pursuit of a Bold Life naturally involves pursuing achievements that enhance our lives and others. Such achievements may target our personal lives, or they may involve our professional careers. But in both cases, achievements provide us with a sense of purpose while adding meaning to our lives.

Likewise, achievements deepen our understanding of the entire human experience and our connection with others—each of these characteristics of achievement highlight why it is an essential Pillar in our quest for boldness.

In focusing on achievement in our lives, we embrace the opportunity to be challenged. These challenges can be overwhelming at times, but they also provide us wonderful opportunities for self-realization and self-actualization.

With every step toward an achievement, we enjoy a chance to use our unique skills, talents, and abilities that make each of us who we are. And by overcoming obstacles along the way, we progressively gain a better appreciation of who we are and the boldness we possess.

Ultimately, achievement, and its pursuit, provide us with experiences that mold our values, perspectives, and lives. Thus, by continually pursuing valued achievements, we can more fully realize a truly Bold Life.

Dr. Laraine Lloyd received her Professional Doctorate in Nursing from the University of Portsmouth in the United Kingdom on July 12, 2019. She received her degree in front of her family and many friends. As it is for anyone receiving such an accomplished degree, it was a special celebratory occasion. A day that Laraine had dreamed about from the time she was 11-years old. This day for Laraine documented achieving an important Bold Life Goal, an accomplishment that would be hers forever.

She had been awarded the highest degree in her profession. What made Dr. Lloyd's story all the more special? She was bestowed her degree just a couple of months before her 70th birthday. She further proves that the road to a Bold Life is accessible to anyone regardless of age or life circumstances.

Her journey was quite the project. Her Bold goal was accomplished as a result of implementing key elements of the Bold Life Formula. When I interviewed Laraine in January 2020, we discussed her journey.

She said, "I never had a true plan, so that is probably why it took me so long. I knew from the time I was 11 that I needed to prove to myself and my father that I was more than how I tested." In Laraine's words, "I failed my 11+, and my age 16 GSCS also had some failure. I viewed myself as smart, yet the world was saying something different." These setbacks made Laraine establish a strong intrinsic goal to prove she was better. Intrinsic or personal goals are an important source of inspiration, sometimes enough, that enable people to accomplish Bold Goals. For Laraine, that personal goal and desire to prove to herself and her family that she could achieve at high academic levels drove her to get her master's degree in 2006. It would take 13 *more years for her to get her doctorate. A couple of aspects of the formula came into play to help Laraine complete her goal.*

Laraine was accepted to the doctoral program in 2011. According to her, she should have completed her doctorate in five to six years. It took her eight. Her story of how she got it done, reminds us of the importance of sharing your commitment with others and having a "fall off your horse plan" with a team ready to assist.

Her field of research involved the study of palliative care patients receiving blood transfusions. She was particularly interested in understanding the care received by palliative patients with short times left to live.

Her goal was to hopefully improve care for these patients as a result of her research and make it easier for people who, in some cases, had only a few weeks to receive care. She interviewed many patients with short times to live who generously gave of their little time left to speak with her. They wanted to help future patients have better experiences, and Laraine's work would do that.

Laraine made promises to these generous patients that their time spent speaking with her would help others in the future. It was a promise that Laraine would keep but not without some challenges.

She had accomplished most of her fieldwork when life events interrupted her work. Her mother became deathly ill, and her daughter had her first child. As a result, from 2014 to 2015, she completely stopped her work to devote her time to her family. So how did Laraine get back on her horse? Two elements of the Bold Life Formula came into play.

Laraine described to me how three of her doctoral program's advisers and supervisors came to her and helped get her back going again after two years away. She said they were instrumental in helping her get going again.

On the Project Bold Life Worksheet My Bold Support Team, there are two exercises concerning support in the formula that people follow to increase their chances of success.

Thankfully, Laraine had both groups in place. She had a support team that helped her when she fell off her horse, and she had made a public commitment to all her patients that she would publish her work for the benefit of future patients.

Laraine said to me, "I really had to complete my doctorate and publish my results. I made promises to so many people that were so close to death that I would try to help others in the future that I could not break that promise. It truly drove me."

So, Laraine, with help from her support team and her public promises, picked up her studies and worked for almost three years to get through to completion. She said it was very hard. She sacrificed family time, playing tennis, and many other opportunities to enjoy life with her family and friends to "lock herself away" and finish her work.

Now Laraine is enjoying life more and also completing the last part of her promise to help and train other caregivers on what she learned from her research at the University of Portsmouth. She is sharing it there and at other medical institutions throughout the U.K.

Laraine has achieved her personal Bold Goal—and kept her promise to her research patients to help others. A Bold Goal well done!

DR LARAINE LLOYD

MY BOLD COMMITMENT
& SUPPORT TEAM

People I have made my Commitment public to   Date Completed
(at least 2)

☐   *THE TERMINALLY ILL I'VE INTERVIEWED*   _____

☐   *FRIENDS AND FAMILY*   _____

☐   _____   _____

People who will help me when I Fall Off the Horse   Date Asked

☐   *DOCTORAL ADVISORS AND SUPERVISORS*   _____

☐   _____   _____

☐   _____   _____

$MBL = M + S/G + Ap$

BOLD LIFE FORMULA WORKSHEET

My Pillar: _ACHIEVEMENT_

My Goal: _TO MAKE A BETTER LIFE FOR MYSELF_

Max had a strong drive for personal achievement, which he saw in a life of opportunity in America. He had a stretch, smart goal to establish himself with his own property and family in America. He accomplished that goal after years of challenges. His Action Plan was not an easy one. Max never saw his mother or father ever again, but he was grateful for his opportunity and thankful for America. He believed it was important to give back and instilled that belief in his children. All five of his sons served in the military during war times, four during World War II, and his youngest during the Korean War.

Max not only altered his life for the better, but he also left a legacy of opportunity for his children, grandchildren, and beyond by following the very hard plan to come to the U.S.

ACHIEVEMENT

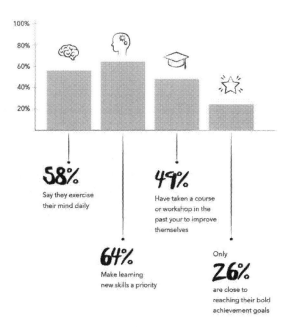

58%
Say they exercise their mind daily

49%
Have taken a course or workshop in the past your to improve themselves

64%
Make learning new skills a priority

Only
26%
are close to reaching their bold achievement goals

Chapter 13 – The Most Coveted Pillar: Career

"Those who succeed and are happy know that the goal is to be authentic and memorable and make a difference, not to be understood and liked by everyone." - Neil Strauss

What do you think about when it pertains to your career? For those seeking a bold life, a career provides a platform to pursue passions, to make a difference, and to attain greater fulfillment. Certainly, a career provides you with the necessary means to have an income. But success in a career offers so much more. Having such an expanded view of career, and the success you want to achieve in your career, play a significant role in your pursuit of boldness regardless of the specific area of interest of work you choose.

For some, true career success may pertain to a specific title or level of recognized accomplishment. Others may define career success as a desired salary level or even the power that they enjoy. Often, these facets of career success are realized in the pursuit of a bold life, but the actual defining feature of true career success exists beyond these facets. For the boldest, career success means attaining superior achievement in your career that is deeply satisfying on a personal level. And it also means attaining a similar level of success in making a difference in society through your career. These aspects of career better define success for those seeking a bold life.

To be bold in your career does not require a specific achievement to be attained or a certain level of influence to be realized. Instead, living boldly through your career simply requires exploring your greatest potential in whatever career pursuits you enjoy. Each of us has unique skills, talents, and interests. Thus, each of us will define boldness in our careers differently. However, some common aspects of this Bold Life Pillar can be readily appreciated.

As we have discussed, an Action Plan is not the only requirement to accomplishing a Bold Goal. The plan must be one where you are prepared to pay the price to achieve it. That price can come in many shapes, not just money. For example, it

could be the price of your time, the price of your passing on other activities, the price to your family or important people in your life are all part of the equation.

Norcross in Changeology has shown that people who take the time to properly prepare before leaping increase their odds of success dramatically. Scott had increased his odds significantly by doing all his research, but the stretch component of his Bold Goal made it truly more amazing! Scott decided to get his MIT Computer Science Degree equivalent in less than one year!

During the planning process, Scott mapped out the 40-course requirements that were part of the MIT degree, final exams and all.

Some were not exact matches, yet he found substitute classes that were close enough to the required curricula. He also figured out how he would take these courses sequentially and what allotted time he had for each course.

Initially, he determined he needed to do a course a week, and he would need to allocate 60 hours per week to each class to get through the materials. He even figured out that he could accelerate the lecture process by running the videos on 1.5x speed!

Scott achieved his Bold Goal on October 1, 2012, when he passed his final course exam. He had completed his Bold Goal and accomplished his MIT Challenge!

Scott's story could have ended there, but it doesn't. Scott's Bold Life had really just begun.

His story and success went viral on social media. Could a guy really learn the equivalent of an entire college degree in a year? Would you hire someone with this education? What would he do next?

Someone from Microsoft reached out to hire him. Remember: Scott was not interested in a job. He had started this with a different goal in mind – to become an entrepreneur – but his success with the MIT Challenge was forcing a course correction. As a result, Scott's Bold Life would enter a new phase. And that was perfectly fine!

The Action Plan portion of the Bold Life Formula Worksheet asks you to lay out the general key steps in your plan. As we saw with the McCurry's and their financial independence goal, the three key action steps were to live frugally, save heavily, and invest wisely. But the specifics of each of these key steps can change from year to year. Scott's plan was coming into shape, but in a different way than he originally had planned.

Heartened by the interest in his story, Scott started to re-think his original Bold Goal. His original intent was to learn to program so that he could develop an app or a product with his newfound knowledge.

But his MIT Challenge had created new opportunities that he could not imagine prior to embarking on his journey. Scott was being asked to consult and speak more and more. So he adjusted his plan.

He decided that the world was seeking him for knowledge sharing and consulting because of his MIT Challenge. His UltraLearning experience was hot, and people wanted to learn more about it. That became his product.

Scott's book was published in 2019 and was a bestseller. His website, in addition to promoting his book, offers several courses, publications and ways to learn his methodologies. He has a successful speaking-, training- and consulting business that helps people meet learning objectives in record time. Scott is no longer a "grey suit." He runs his own business and enjoys choosing his hours, clients and how he wants to work.

Another Bold Goal in the Career Pillar accomplished!

Another thing worth noting about Scott and the achievement of his Bold Goal: his goal changed over time (and with the success of his UltraLearning endeavor). That's perfectly fine when that happens!

KNOW YOUR WHY
GOAL REFINER

▶ Every goal needs to be distilled down to its most basic motivation, for only in those "why" questions can true inspiration be found.

Start by putting your goal in the top box. Then move down to the box below it and answer the question "Why?" Then do it again, then again. Since the aim is to gain a better understanding of your motivations, your "Ultimate Why" will be the most distilled understanding of your goal.

What is your goal?

> ACCOMPLISHING SOMETHING IS IMPORTANT TO ME

But why is that important?

> BECAUSE WITHOUT THAT SENSE OF FULFILLMENT, I FEEL I'VE ACCOMPLISHED NOTHING

But why is that important?

> BECAUSE I NEED WORK THAT FULFILLS ME

Why is this important to you?

> BECAUSE WORKING IN AN OFFICE IS NOT SATISFYING

The Ultimate Why

> TO BECOME AN ENTREPRENEUR

PBL = Pi + (S/G) + Ap

Ultimately, the constant refinement of a Bold Goal is just the nature of the beast. After all, we all live in a dynamic world rife with change. Having the flexibility to change along with it is a good thing.

I met Thaddeus Bullard at the Synapse Innovation Conference in March of 2018. He had agreed to an interview and Dawna Stone, from Bold Business, would be the lead interviewer. As I listened to his interview, I was struck by Thaddeus' genuine care to help others. His story helped me understand his "why".

The world may know Thaddeus Bullard by his World Wrestling Entertainment stage name "Titus O'Neil", but that star status as a professional athlete came after a rough start in life and a long, hard road to overcome the hurdles in his way.

Thaddeus' mother, Daria, was raped by her mother's boyfriend at age 11 and gave birth to him a year later. Without a father figure, Thaddeus grew up drawn to the streets. During his interview he shared, "I was labeled a kid that will be dead or in jail by the time I was 16-years old."[25] Instead, he received an opportunity to go to Florida Sheriffs Boys Ranch, an organization that took in at-risk youth and motivated them to create a sense of direction for themselves.

Soon, Bullard's life took a turn for the better. At 12, he remarked that a stranger told him, "I love you and I believe in you." This statement from a

---

[25] For more on Titus O'Neil, I refer you to the Bold Business story and video interview at https://www.boldbusiness.com/human-achievement/how-can-your-business-persevere-against-all-odds/

random stranger changed the course of his life. The importance of a support team is critical to success. Thaddeus, to this point, had no one to support him and care for him. That support made all the difference for young Thaddeus.

He went on to become an outstanding football player in high school and received an athletic scholarship from the University of Florida in the late 90s. He also played for the Florida Gators and the Tampa Bay Storm.

Bullard then moved on to debut on the WWE in 2010 and has since then maintained an illustrious career as a wrestler with the name Titus O'Neil. Bullard did not give in to the low expectations and vowed never to give up on himself. He made a Bold Goal for himself as a kid and went from someone with a dodgy future to someone with a fruitful career as a pro athlete.

In 2020, Titus continues his passionate work helping other disadvantaged youths. His inspirational pillar is well defined by this statement. "People invested in me when they had nothing to gain in return. Every day is an opportunity to return the favor for others."[26]

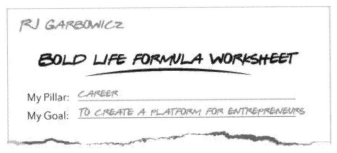

RJ GARBOWICZ

BOLD LIFE FORMULA WORKSHEET

My Pillar: *CAREER*
My Goal: *TO CREATE A PLATFORM FOR ENTREPRENEURS*

RJ Garbowicz is living a Bold Life, and it stems from his dogged pursuit of a Bold Goal in the Career Pillar. Specifically, he's worked hard as an entrepreneur to create WebTalk[27], a platform that could help other entrepreneurs (and businesses) throughout the world.

I met with RJ over coffee, and he agreed to a little Q and A. We then talked about his motivations and some of the procedural nitty-gritty of getting his business to the brink of success. But what really stuck out is how RJ admitted that, because of his laser-like focus on success, other aspects of his life have suffered.

What was the inspiration for you to start WebTalk?

---

[26] To read more about Thaddeus, check out his book, *There's No Such Thing as a Bad Kid: How I Went from Stereotype to Prototype*, ECW Press 2019

[27] To learn more about Webtalk, check out: https://www.webtalk.co/o

RJ: I've been building tech companies since I was a teenager, and in my previous venture, I discovered a gamification digital marketing strategy that was extremely powerful. It was so powerful that it made a product that was buggy and not ready for market yet a cash flow positive company within nine months of launching it.

This was when I knew it was time to think big after discovering the holy grail of internet marketing. It was a marketing discovery that could potentially make any product successful. I then set out to raise money for my previous venture to make a pivot to go big and ended up selling out to our lead investor.

That money seed funded Webtalk and allowed me to put my big plan into action as a new venture. The plan was financially motivated at the core, as Webtalk has the potential to generate substantial profits, but it was focused on generating profits by solving real problems I dealt with daily.

I wanted to build a product I'm passionate about that I would use every day to solve my own problems (as a UX Architect and Designer myself that's no easy feat), and I wanted a mission that our team could hang their hats on every night knowing their daily efforts were helping to change the world for the better.

Building an all-in-one relationship and brand management platform to power the fast-growing Gig Economy with a mission to help the world create more success checked all of the boxes.

It was a big goal with a huge financial opportunity, it was a mission our team could be proud of, and it was an area where all of the founders had the experience to contribute. We are entrepreneurs in the Gig economy, building a platform for entrepreneurs in the Gig economy to create more success.

What year did you begin?

RJ: In 2011, I began designing the app and making the plan. In 2013 I launched a prototype that had immediate traction proving the concept before the pilot software, made in India, bottlenecked from a traffic overload. In March 2015, I had recruited the founding team and raised funds needed to build a beta production version. In 2017 we launched a closed beta. In 2018 we launched an invite-only open beta with mobile compatibility, and in 2020 we plan to launch v1.0 with open enrollment on all devices;

web, mobile web, iOS and Android. As an all-in-one platform, we had a very long R&D cycle.

Did you have what I refer to as a broad Building Block Plan? If so, what were those key building blocks?

RJ: Yes, of course, and it was quite a detailed plan due to the nature of building a consolidation platform with market-defining technologies. The goal was to automate everything using technology. Sales, marketing, and support are the most critical to automate to allow Webtalk to rapidly grow on its own revenue without raising billions of dollars from venture capitalists to cover the data management and support costs.

Phase 1 is to plan, phase 2 is to prove the model, phase 3 invest into a scalable production version, phase 4 is to test the free technologies, phase 5 is to test the revenue technologies, phase 6 is to test the marketing and support technologies, phase 7 is to duplicate the production-ready product on all devices and phase 8 is to launch a PR campaign to kick off a big viral growth wave.

What is your Bold Goal for yourself as it relates to career/Webtalk?

RJ: Aside from making Webtalk a unicorn, I would like to create over a million success stories of how Webtalk helped 1M+ people create financial freedom in the Gig Economy, and I would like to see just as many success stories be created from the amount of people whose lives we improved from our 10% charity pledge.

How have you balanced family and work during your journey?

RJ: The truth is I haven't, and I believe that obtaining balance as an entrepreneur is a myth. In order to do anything big, I believe you have to give it your all 110% of the time and make big sacrifices to achieve your goals.

You recently reached 5.0 million users, and it took some time to finally get there. What is the ultimate goal?

RJ: We actually have surpassed 5.0M users, and yes, it did take time, but that was entirely intentional. We have been controlling our growth as we complete Beta testing.

When we opened the door without controls, it exposed several weaknesses. We had invested so much on bringing in new users that we overlooked the critical aspect of keeping out bad users during our development. It took us an extra year to build and deploy new services to keep out bad actors and keep our community safe.

Do you have a support team to turn to when you feel you are off track? Can you share a story on how they have personally helped you through some of the challenges?

RJ: Since we have five highly experienced founders, most things get resolved within our weekly founder meetings as we are each other's support. Plus, we maintain open daily communication through our team management tools to get through the small issues quickly. Outside of the team, I have a large network of successful entrepreneurs I can turn to when I need high-level advice and support.

Was there a particular time you believed your goal was in trouble? How did you pull yourself through it?

RJ: Fundraising for any new venture is extremely difficult and time-consuming. Raising nearly $9MM for a large startup project seemed impossible by many, including myself at times, and at times it was. We went through several gaps in funding, where I had to mortgage my home and max out my credit cards to survive and keep the company alive.

Project Bold Life is about living Bold and looking to accomplish something you are personally proud of. What is that Bold Goal you are looking to achieve?

RJ: My goal is to leave a big enough impact on the world that it will change its course for the better forever. Webtalk's mission is to help the world create more success, and we live and breathe it in everything we do from our products to sharing revenue with our members, to our 10% charity donation pledge.

When our entire product roadmap has been fulfilled, I truly believe we will have created the most trusted global ecosystem to do business, and when that happens, it will reduce wasteful spending and speed up innovation, ultimately helping the world create more success.

CAREER

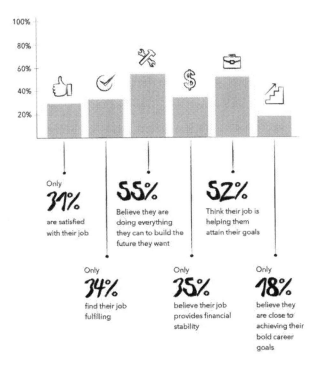

Only
31%
are satisfied
with their job

55%
Believe they are
doing everything
they can to build the
future they want

52%
Think their job is
helping them
attain their goals

Only
34%
find their job
fulfilling

Only
35%
believe their job
provides financial
stability

Only
18%
believe they
are close to
achieving their
bold career
goals

Research based on Project Bold Life Assessment at BoldLifeScore.com

Chapter 14 – The Most Confusing Pillar: Finances

"Finance is not merely about making money. It's about achieving our deep goals and protecting the fruits of our labor. It's about stewardship and therefore about achieving the good society." –
Robert J. Shiller

When it comes to finances, the pursuit of money can create problems for many people. Earning money can consume every effort rather than pursuing other activities that make your life valued and bold.

Likewise, money can taint how you perceive the value of other things in life. Some aspects of life may be highly valuable yet not be assigned a high monetary worth in society, and vice versa. For these reasons, money, and managing it, can either enhance or undermine our life's journey and our efforts to be our very best.

Money itself is not a bad thing, of course. In essence, money is simply a resource that can enable us to achieve various goals in life. Access to money provides opportunities that might not otherwise exist.

Similarly, a lack of access has been shown to predispose individuals to illness, poor health, and other personal and social risks.

Each of us needs money at some level to survive, and therefore, it is important that we know how to manage our finances well. And at the same time, we must appreciate its role (and limits) that it plays in our life.

Financial stewardship is an important part of living a Bold Life. This essential Pillar deserves our attention because effectively managing our finances opens doors to excellence in many ways.

Not only does this provide opportunities for accountability and responsibility, but it also offers a chance to give back, invest in ourselves, and make the world a better place. Thus, properly managing our finances also helps us better pursue other Bold Life Pillars.

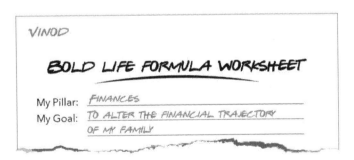

In 1996, I traveled to India for a recruiting trip for my client, Boeing Aircraft. Boeing was looking to build a first-rate aerospace engineering team for a new aircraft they would be designing, the Boeing 777. Traveling with me were recruiters

and executives from my company and four Boeing engineers. The team's job was to interview and hire first-rate aerospace engineers for this project. We were looking to hire about 200 engineers and would be interviewing in Mumbai and Bangalore for a week.

The response by candidates was amazing. Hundreds of people submitted resumes to us, and we had given out 300-plus invites to come for interviews. Some candidates traveled a full day or more across India to have an opportunity to get a job offer from us. The job would be in the U.S., and we would travel the future employees in for what was estimated to be about a two-three-year work assignment. This was before the popular talent shows, but the lines of people were impressive. People without invites were showing up!

As CEO, my job was to make sure our client and team were all functioning well and to assist with bottlenecks. At times candidates needed help with the next steps and what interview stations they needed to be at.

I knew this was an exciting time for potential employees, but what happened to me one afternoon in Bangalore with one of the candidates moved me in a way that was unforgettable.

Vinod was a man in his late 50's who had a Master's degree and Ph.D. in aeronautical engineering. He was a published engineer, and his credentials were incredible. Boeing and our team, after interviewing him, were all very impressed. An offer of employment would be issued.

Vinod was being escorted from his interviews to an area where his employment paperwork would be completed. He was clearly emotional when I first looked into his eyes when he was walking towards me. He asked the recruiter if he could speak with me. She said yes.

At that point, Vinod came up to me and fell to his knees and began to cry. He reached for my hand and held it as I tried to speak with him. He said, "Thank you. Thank you. Thank you." Through his tears and sobs, he said, "You have changed my life forever. You have changed my Family's lives forever and my next generations of family. I am humbled by this opportunity."

Vinod viewed himself as the luckiest man in the world.

I asked him after he calmed himself why he was so emotional. He explained that he was employed in India at the equivalent U.S. wage of 22 cents per hour. He was only earning $40 a month. Our offer would be for $30 per hour plus overtime $45 per hour. One overtime hour would be more than he made in a month! We were expecting him to work 60-hour weeks. He would make more in a week than he would make in four years! His 100-week expected assignment would be worth 400 years of work.

He told me that his earnings would be used to help his family for generations.

I said to him that no thanks were in order. I thanked him for applying and preparing so well throughout his life. It was his commitment to learning and study that created this opportunity. We would pay him the same as all of our employees regardless of their country of origin or citizenship status. That he was very deserving of this opportunity, and we would be fortunate to have his talents on this project.

Vinod was a superstar employee and worked until completion of the project. His long and humble commitment to learning enabled him to deliver a Bold Life for himself and his family for generations – a Bold Goal achieved in the Finances Pillar!

FINANCES

Only
35%
feel financially
stable

42%
Are putting
money towards
retirement

59%
Are less than
good at setting
aside money for
emergencies/rainy
days

47%
Believe their
debt is
manageable

45%
Are spending
less money than
they make

Only
14%
believe they are
close to achieving
their bold finance
goals

Chapter 15 – The Most Sought After Pillar: Relationships

"Each friend represents a world in us, a world possibly not born until they arrive, and it is only by this meeting that a new world is born." – Anais Nin

The value that relationships add to your life cannot be understated. More than anything else in our lives, being able to connect with others, and enjoying a sense of belonging, enhances our well-being. As a result, investing in relationships and the skills required to maintain them are important.

Such efforts not only pay huge dividends in success and personal health, but they also provide deeper meaning to our lives. In fact, the ability to successfully form lasting and trusting relationships with others increases our ability to excel in all the other Bold Life Pillars.

Relationships are essential for leading a Bold Life for a number of reasons. On a personal level, relationships help us better understand who we are while providing chances for us to continually improve and grow.

In addition, these types of relationships help us develop intimacy with others, which allows us to express ourselves better and enjoy deeper human connections.

In a broader sense, relationships introduce situations where we can make positive impacts on the lives of others. This extends beyond the relationship with individuals to those with entire communities and even society at large. As a result, we can be bold in many areas of our life when we progressively seek meaningful relationships.

Several steps can be taken to help you develop relational skills. Notably, communication skills, empathy, emotional intelligence, and other talents increase the chance that the relationships in your life will be successful.

But most importantly is your commitment to making relationships a priority in your life.

Each of us has the capacity to enjoy strong relationships and their benefits in our lives. By simply investing in the efforts required, you can foster powerful connections with others that are certain to make your life bolder and better.

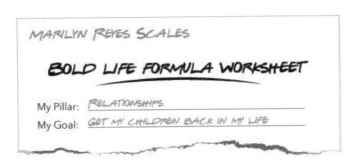

MARILYN REYES SCALES

BOLD LIFE FORMULA WORKSHEET

My Pillar: RELATIONSHIPS
My Goal: GET MY CHILDREN BACK IN MY LIFE

I walked into the event room at SubCulture, 45 Bleecker St in New York City around 5:45 pm on

March 16, 2017. My company,
www.BoldBusiness.com/publication/, was the
media partner for an event put on by
www.impactnyc.org , a New York-based issues
and think tank that creates quality discussion
about the biggest issues of the day. The hall sat
about 250, and it was pretty empty as the
discussion was to begin at 7 pm. The event that
night was addressing an important topic, "Impact
Prisons 2017: The Future of the Correctional
System."

My role that evening was to interview some of the
speakers prior to the event and help frame out
the key messages for the post-event reporting we
would do. I was there with a camera crew and
support.

I have to admit that I was not very up to date on
correctional system reform issues prior to getting
involved with the event, but the night for me and
the standing-room-only crowd that would later
come in would be moved and enlightened.
ImpactNYC had assembled a very thoughtful
group of speakers and participants for the
evening. The list was impressive and included
Cyrus Vance Jr., NYC District Attorney, Vikrant
Reddy, Senior Research Fellow - Charles Koch
Institute, Sister Tesa Fitzgerald-Founder Hour
Children, and Lina Tetelbaum, Wachtell, Lipton,
Rosen & Katz.

One participant not on the initial speaker roster
was Marilyn Reyes Scales, a convicted felon who
had served time in prison for drugs in the mid-
1990s and was released in January of 1997.
Although she had served her time 20 years ago,
her story and the story of another of her panel
participants who had also spent time in prison,
James L. Eleby Jr., Refoundry Entrepreneur,
highlighted the many challenges people face after

"paying their price to society." Marilyn's story really resonated with the crowd.

Some people in the corrections industry say the first thing men do after prison is look for jobs while women look for their families. Marilyn wanted both. The challenges, though, are very real.

The many difficulties for people to rebuild their lives after their release are starkly ever-present. Getting a job? Very hard. Repairing relationships? Also, very hard. Finding a place to live? Very difficult if the family will not take you in. Staying off drugs? Very challenging. Avoiding depression and victim mentality? Very, very hard. Living a Bold Life? Most would say impossible!

Marilyn has a strong personality and is a passionate communicator. She chose to pursue a Bold Life. She wanted to get her family back and make a difference in the world

When she got released, Marilyn said her relationships with her oldest daughters were severely broken. She wanted them back. Since she was a former heavy drug user and now a convicted felon, her children were very skeptical of her.

She had some simple goals: "Get food for my family. Stay out of Prison. Stay Drug-Free."

It was not easy. She said, "Society sees me as a felon. I did not want to go backward. To get food was a struggle. Legally."

On the stage that night, one of the most moving moments occurred when she proudly announced that she had been free of drugs for 20 years and had her family back. She was also very proud of the fact that she had been asked to be a godmother for three children.

She had earned respect back with friends and family. Her Bold Goal of getting her family back was her most satisfying accomplishment.

*Marilyn's story highlights the many prices people pay after serving their time. I had interviewed Vikrant Reddy, Senior Research Fellow at the **Charles Koch Institute**[28], prior to the event, and the Koch Institute has been working passionately to change the system of incarceration in the U.S.*

---

[28] https://www.charleskochinstitute.org/

Vikrant had spoken about the many long-term problems people face after release from prison. He opened my eyes prior to the event, and Marilyn's comments that night were directly on point. The percentage of the population in U.S prisons is the second highest in the world. Seychelles is the highest, but they have a lot of Somali pirates. The United States is truly an outlier when it comes to incarceration.[29]

Marilyn did not realize it, but she perfectly laid out her Building Block Plan on how to get her family back when she exited prison. She was looking to take the right road, the bold road.

The building block steps were:

- *Get a job*
- *Stay off drugs*
- *Be able to legally provide home and shelter for her family*
- *Earn back the respect of her family and community*

---

[29] For more on Vikrant's work and his video interview, go to https://www.boldbusiness.com/society/charles-koch-institute-on-prison-system/

Bold Goal: To get her family back.

Since getting her family back was Marilyn's primary objective, we'll classify her Bold Goal as one in the Relationships Pillar.

If she were to have filled out a Building Block Plan Worksheet, it would have looked something like this:

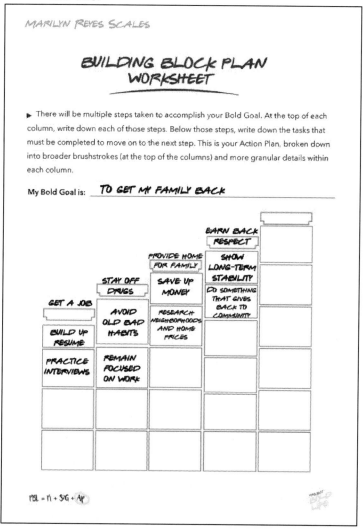

MARILYN REYES SCALES

BUILDING BLOCK PLAN WORKSHEET

▶ There will be multiple steps taken to accomplish your Bold Goal. At the top of each column, write down each of those steps. Below those steps, write down the tasks that must be completed to move on to the next step. This is your Action Plan, broken down into broader brushstrokes (at the top of the columns) and more granular details within each column.

My Bold Goal is: __TO GET MY FAMILY BACK__

				EARN BACK RESPECT	
			PROVIDE HOME FOR FAMILY	SHOW LONG-TERM STABILITY	
		STAY OFF DRUGS	SAVE UP MONEY	DO SOMETHING THAT GIVES BACK TO COMMUNITY	
	GET A JOB	AVOID OLD BAD HABITS	RESEARCH NEIGHBORHOODS AND HOME PRICES		
	BUILD UP RESUME	REMAIN FOCUSED ON WORK			
	PRACTICE INTERVIEWS				

BGL = M + SG + AP

One important aspect of recovery and thriving again for people with addiction is a principle in the 12-step program. It is AA's 12th step, and it refers to carrying the message to others.

Marilyn embraced this idea and worked for years on a "Remove the Box" initiative in NYC. "Remove the Box" refers to the idea of changing the law to remove a question on an employment application that asks, "Have you ever been convicted or committed a felony?"

That question effectively quashes potential opportunities for people who have served their time. Many companies simply will not hire any ex-felons, regardless of their crime or how long ago it may have occurred. Marilyn shared that her years-long effort was finally accomplished in NYC when Mayor Bill DeBlasio signed "Remove the Box" into law. Marilyn was beaming proudly on stage that night.

She said, "I was there for the signing. I even was given the pen the Mayor used to sign the law into effect. I have the pen!" Marilyn became a celebrity in the corrections reform movement in NYC as a result.

More importantly, Marilyn had earned back respect in her community and with her family. She was very appreciative of all the support she received through her journey. She reinforced the importance of a support team in order to build a successful life.

Marilyn had, 20 years earlier, walked out of prison a felon and former drug addict, and that evening she was a drug-free, self-sufficient and respected community organizer who had earned *back the respect and love of her family and community.*

Her story proves without question that anyone, regardless of circumstances, can live a Bold Life. Let me say that again. **Anyone can live a Bold Life, regardless of circumstances!** *Marilyn's Bold Goal and accomplishments inspired everyone that evening and beyond!*

AMY CHUA

BOLD LIFE FORMULA WORKSHEET

My Pillar: RELATIONSHIPS

My Goal: TO HELP MY KIDS SUCCEED

Sophia and her sister Lulu grew up in a household of Bold parents. From the time Sophia was young, her parents were on a mission to teach her the important principles of passion for learning, hard work and setting goals.

From all practical perspectives, Sophia and her sister developed into two very accomplished women with strong relationships with their parents. The values of hard work and academic achievement are now fully part of them. Sophia, now 27, would end up going to Harvard for her B.A. on an R.O.T.C. scholarship and then get her law degree from Yale. The younger sister, Lulu, age 22, also earned her B.A. from Harvard in 2018 and is a law student in the Harvard Law Class of 2022.

In June 2019, it was announced Sophia was appointed to be an intern for Supreme Court Justice Brett Kavanaugh for the October 2019 to June 2020 term. A Bold accomplishment indeed! For Sophia! And for Sophia's parents. Bold parenting played an important role.

The building block plan that Sophie and Lulu's parents followed was instrumental in driving the academic success of the two sisters.

It included:
1. No TV until college
2. No playdates or sleepovers
3. A commitment to A's only in the core subjects
4. Musical practice up to six hours per day.

That's a very strong plan that many parents might find too strict and rigid. Overly strict child-rearing is not a popular idea, particularly in Western culture.

For any parent who wants academic success for their children, Sophia and Lulu's story would logically generate a very high degree of interest. And it did. Their story became a best-selling book. The book coined a new phrase, "Tiger Mom." Sophia and Lulu grew up in a fishbowl as a result.

Their mom, Amy Chua, published "Battle Hymn of the Tiger Mother" in January of 2011. The book was on the New York Times bestseller list from January 30 to April 10, 2011. The book created lots of controversy as to the right approach to parenting.

The intent of the book was to share a memoir on Amy's child-rearing approach and her evolution. She eventually lightened up on rebellious LuLu. She did not intend for the book to be a "how-to" book. Amy did believe strict Chinese parenting styles were more effective in bringing up children, and she evolved as a result of her personal experience with her daughters.

Chua published excerpts from her book in a piece "Why Chinese Mothers Are Superior" in The Wall Street Journal on January 8, 2011. It was intended to generate buzz and sales. It did both.

Attitudes about the child-rearing plan were very mixed, with many people criticizing Amy for the discipline she had enforced.

However, when it came to getting results, opinions shifted. According to a poll taken by the Wall Street Journal, "two-thirds of respondents voted that the 'Demanding Eastern' parenting model is better than the 'Permissive Western' model."[30]

For the past nine years since the book's publication, Sophia and Lulu have had a very "public childhood." Effectively, their mother made a public commitment to have her daughters grow up to become very successful and well adjusted.

By all accounts, she has been successful. As outlined in previous sections, public commitments

---

[30] https://blogs.wsj.com/ideas-market/2011/01/13/the-tiger-mother-responds-to-readers

are an important component of a successful action plan in the Formula. Amy did not realize it, but she increased the chances of her daughters' success by writing her book.

The pressure on Sophia, Lulu and Amy was clearly on. Now, nine years after the book publication, Sophia and Lulu are very accomplished ladies. Wow!

Many have wondered how they adapted to all the attention from their mother's book.

In an April 2016 Nextshark interview, Sophia shared thoughts about her relationship with her mother and the impact the discipline had on her. "' I'm fine. I'm really happy. I'm awesome!' I've given up trying to give people logical arguments about why I'm OK."[31]

Also, Lulu, who did not watch TV until college, had the most difficulty with the approach. She said in a recent Slate interview, "As I've gotten older, I've realized that my mom and I are increasingly similar... I think a lot of people assume that my mom is the kind of person who would be upset if I got a bad grade on something, but that's really not at all how she operates. She always says, 'Have no regrets. If you work really hard and you have no regrets, you don't think that you could've done more, then you should be happy.'"

---

[31] https://nextshark.com/sophia-chua-rubenfeld-interview/

*In a June 2019 interview with Heavy.com, Sophia
said she plans to be a Tiger Mom someday
herself.[32]*

*Setting goals, public commitments and a detailed
action plan all part of the Tiger Mom program
and part of the Bold Life Formula!*

Parents, take note!

---

[32] https://heavy.com/news/2019/06/sophia-chua-rubenfeld/

RELATIONSHIPS

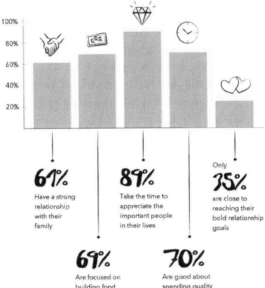

61%

Have a strong
relationship
with their
family

89%

Take the time to
appreciate the
important people
in their lives

Only
35%

are close to
reaching their
bold relationship
goals

69%

Are focused on
building fond
memories with
family and friends

70%

Are good about
spending quality
time with friends

Research based on Project Bold Life Assessment at BoldLifeScore.com

Chapter 16 – The Most Overlooked Pillar: Giving Back

"The best way to find yourself is to lose yourself in the service of others." – Mahatma Gandhi

Among all the Bold Life Pillars, the Pillar of giving back is among one of the most important and the most powerful. When we choose to give back, we are not simply making the decision to share ourselves with others. We are actually making a choice of empowerment and strength. Certainly, giving back provides support, resources, and strength to those receiving. But at the same time, giving back empowers and strengthens ourselves as well as our communities.

For this reason, integrating ways to give back into your life is essential when trying to be your absolute best.

Giving back can be accomplished in a variety of ways. From a traditional perspective, giving back may involve contributing charitable donations, volunteering to help in a community project, or donating your time to help out at the local food kitchen. And yet plenty of non-traditional opportunities to give back exist as well.

For example, choosing to become a public-school teacher naturally involves giving back, or working as a physician at a free community clinic involves similar efforts. Likewise, you may serve as a little league soccer coach or lead a community running club. Each of these activities is an example of giving back, regardless of whether they fall into a traditional or non-traditional concept.

The pursuit of a Bold Life can be greatly enhanced by seeking ways to combine passion with giving back. When we identify such passions, we can tap into tremendous energies in helping others as well as society.

I first met Henry Stifel in my NYC office in 2017. He had come to be interviewed for a story I was working on about the work of the Christopher and Dana Reeve Foundation.

Henry came into the interview room in a wheelchair, his mode of mobility since 1983, when he lost his ability to walk in a car accident that paralyzed him. Henry was only 19-years old on the night of his fateful accident and has spent his adulthood in a wheelchair. I was very moved by the interview.

Henry shared with me the story of how the original name of the Christopher and Dana Reeve Foundation was the Stifel Foundation[33], named after him; how he and his family had worked tirelessly for many years to help people who suffer from spinal cord injury; how Christopher Reeve came to be the namesake and leader of the foundation and more importantly about the life-altering work they were doing. Little did I know what a powerhouse Henry is and has been!

You see, Henry had made the decision after his accident to live a very Bold Life.

---

[33] For more on the Reeve Foundation, check out: https://www.christopherreeve.org/

Henry's passion and drive to help others through his work with the Foundation were creating an impact in the world, and an even larger impact for the world of five million people in wheelchairs.

From Henry and CEO Peter Wilderotter of the Christopher Reeve Foundation, I learned firsthand that day about the "Big Idea." The Foundation was committed to eliminating wheelchairs and solving the problem of spinal cord injury once and for all.

The Big Idea: People with spinal cord injuries, through the help of technology and science, will walk again. Wow!

During my interview, Henry spoke passionately about the research and progress being made.

He took me through aspects of the spine and how research is showing that the right type of neurological stimulation to the spine has enabled people to get many of their lost functioning skills back.

I was shown a video of how people were regaining use of their hands and motor skills, including the ability to move their legs, resulting in steps.

While talking with Henry, I did not see a man in a wheelchair. I saw a man living a Bold Life, lost in the service of others, who simply would not or could not let any personal circumstances of his get in the way of achieving his Bold Life Goal. A man on a mission.

Henry has worked on this very personal Project Bold Life Goal for over 25 years.

His enthusiasm for it continues, and the breakthroughs that Henry's work has helped underwrite and enable are on the verge of massive breakthroughs.

His Bold Life follows all steps of the formula, the giving back Pillar, specific and stretch goals, and an Action Plan that he has followed for 25 years.

A truly inspirational Bold Life story.

Giving back to Henry is an important Bold Life Pillar.

FATHER SIRICO

BOLD LIFE FORMULA WORKSHEET

My Pillar: GIVING BACK

My Goal: TO CHANGE CHURCH DOCTRINE OF THE VALUE OF WEALTH

Father Robert Sirico was born in Brooklyn, NY, on June 23, 1951. Raised Catholic by Italian parents, he led a typical life of youth in the '50s and '60s. In his teenage years, Robert left New York and moved to California to go to college. He received his B.A. in English from the University of Southern California in 1981 just shortly before his 30th birthday. Robert clearly had wandered in his early years, both geographically and intellectually. He stated in an interview on C-Span on May 23, 2012: "I suppose the fact that I spent time on the left of the political spectrum isn't the surprising thing. I mean, I'm a New Yorker; I'm a child of the '60s; I went to seminary in the early 1980s, when a baptized form of Marxism was next to godliness. When you take all of that into account, my sojourn on the left has about it almost the inevitability of Marxist dialectic. What most people find surprising isn't that I was once a card-carrying lefty but that, despite my background, I somehow ended up as a passionate defender of the free economy, of liberty and limited government, of a traditional understanding of culture and morality, of all of those things that America's Founders held dear and that our country is now in danger of losing."

From the seeds of his intellectual journey through religion and economic philosophy came Father Sirico's Project Bold Life inspiration. Father Sirico has passionately worked to educate fellow clergy and people of faith to understand and embrace the moral philosophy of individual freedom, market freedom, and the evils of socialism. He has created a movement teaching the compatibility – Father Sirico would say necessity – of religion and economic freedom. He co-founded the Acton Institute for the Study of Religion and Liberty in 1990, along with Kris Alan Mauren in Grand Rapids, MI, to help him with his Bold Life project.[34]

The event later that evening was another step in the action plan for Acton and Father Sirico. That step? Bring their message of liberty and religion to more people in a repeatable way. The film was

---

[34] For more on the Acton Institute, check out https://www.acton.org/

Acton's first highly-produced video that could be used to educate more people about its work. Increasing public awareness of Acton's message was an important goal of the film.

Our dinner became, to me, an event as well. I had the opportunity to engage in a lively and insightful discussion about the call of entrepreneurialism, religion and economic philosophy all in one swoop. This was not your typical dinner. It was the perfect prep for the night ahead. Call of the Entrepreneur tells the story of three entrepreneurs, all from different backgrounds. It highlights the positive role creators and leaders of businesses have in our lives and societies. It helps explain the integral role of business success to the success of everyday people. The film's message is very different from what Father Sirico was taught in seminary and what most people are taught or think about business leaders. Over dinner, we discussed various messages and ideas we wanted to get across after the showing of the film.

The evening was a grand success, and the crowd enjoyed the film and the dialogue afterward. The messages for the night were clear. Entrepreneurialism is a calling and should be supported by all. Freedom to start a company and enjoy the fruits of your work are moral concepts that need to be fervently protected. The best way to help the poor is to start a company, help grow the economic pie, and to protect freedom. And finally, religious faith, care for the poor, individual freedom and support of entrepreneurialism are a dynamic combination that serves to make the world a better, more moral place for all.

Since that night in 2008, Father Sirico's work has continued. He authored a bestselling book,

"Defending the Free Market: The Moral Case for a Free Economy"[35] in 2012 that takes on important questions that are even more important today, questions such as:

Q: What is the best way to help the poor? (A: Start a business.)

Q: Why does charity work but welfare doesn't?

Q: Why can't we have freedom without a free economy?

Q: Why is "blaming the rich guy" a morally and economically corrupt argument that inevitably leads to disaster for all?

On a theological basis, Father Sirico's work has received important recognition. He has worked to educate the Church and clergy on economics and liberty, and their relation to religious teaching. He has also helped the clergy understand the destruction Marxism and socialism have caused for the world and its moral teaching.

He has been instrumental in building upon John Paul II's encyclical Centesimus annus, published in 1991. Father Sirico educates people on how freedom and virtue are both necessary conditions for a flourishing society, and how neither by itself is sufficient.

The work of the Acton Institute places a dignified vision of the human person at the center of economic analysis and defends the compatibility of religious principles with individual liberty and free markets. He has consistently made a case for freedom and how it makes aid to the poor more effective.

---

[35] Father Robert Sirico, *Defending the Free Market: The Moral Case for a Free Economy* (Regnery Publishing, 2012)

Father Sirico also supports approaches that "call on the capacities of the poor" and are supported by the free choices of people (i.e., charity) and not forced by government decree (i.e., welfare). These principles have led to better thinking about how the clergy and religion can do their work and improve the world.

Project Bold Life's message incorporates this part of Father Sirico's message. We all, regardless of circumstances, have the capacity to achieve bold accomplishments. A system that does not reinforce optimistic possibilities and personal responsibility for one's life is otherwise morally deficient.

From humble beginnings, the Acton Institute has become a powerhouse think tank and educational center.

It started with a Bold Goal. It is hard to imagine a priest in Michigan is changing how people all over the world think about helping the poor, the moral dimensions of markets, and the interrelation between religion and liberty, but it's happened - a Bold Goal indeed!

Father Sirico has accomplished much, and he continues living his passion.

I am certain much more success will follow.

If Father Sirico were to have used the Project Bold Life methodology in determining his Bold Goals and subsequent course of action, he would've likely begun with the Pillar Ranker to iron out what was important to him—and when that particular goal would best be tackled.

It would look something like this:

FATHER SIRICO

PILLAR RANKER

	IMPORTANCE	TIMING	WHY
HEALTH	○ Very Important ○ Important ☒ Not Important	○ Now ○ Later ○ Much Later	_____
FINANCES	○ Very Important ○ Important ☒ Not Important	○ Now ○ Later ○ Much Later	_____
CAREER	○ Very Important ○ Important ☒ Not Important	○ Now ○ Later ○ Much Later	_____
ACHIEVEMENTS	○ Very Important ☒ Important ○ Not Important	○ Now ☒ Later ○ Much Later	TO ACHIEVE SOMETHING GREAT FOR THE GREATER GOOD IS ITS OWN REWARD
RELATIONSHIPS	○ Very Important ○ Important ☒ Not Important	○ Now ○ Later ○ Much Later	_____
GIVING BACK	☒ Very Important ○ Important ○ Not Important	☒ Now ○ Later ○ Much Later	BECAUSE REFRAMING CHURCH VIEWS ON WEALTH CAN OPEN MORE TO HELPING
EXPERIENCES	○ Very Important ○ Important ☒ Not Important	○ Now ○ Later ○ Much Later	_____

- HEALTH — Both physical and mental well-being
- FINANCES — The fiscal wherewithal to survive and thrive
- CAREER — Work that fulfills
- ACHIEVEMENTS — Accomplishments you are proud of
- RELATIONSHIPS — Family, friends and everything in between
- GIVING BACK — Charity and volunteering
- EXPERIENCES — Those memorable things that make life worth living

IMPORTANCE
VI – Very Important   I – Important

TIMING
Now   Later   Much Later

$PBL = fi + SfG + Af$

GIVING BACK

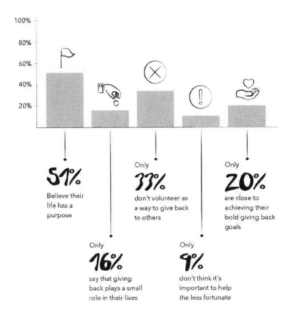

51%
Believe their
life has a
purpose

Only
33%
don't volunteer as
a way to give back
to others

Only
20%
are close to
achieving their
bold giving back
goals

Only
16%
say that giving
back plays a small
role in their lives

Only
9%
don't think it's
important to help
the less fortunate

Chapter 17 – The Most Enlightening Pillar: Experiences

"People grow through experience if they meet life honestly and courageously. This is how character is built." - Eleanor Roosevelt

How do you define experiences? Many would describe experiences as events that occur throughout life that affect how we think, feel, and see the world. From this point of view, experiences play a significant role in who we are and who we will become. It is, therefore, not surprising that the experiences we choose can help guide us in our pursuit of a Bold Life. By consciously incorporating specific experiences in your life, you can better guide your growth, development, and progress along the way. In doing so, you increase the likelihood of attaining your life goals and your ultimate fulfillment.

Naturally, you cannot arrange all your life experiences exactly as you would like. But you can choose to include some experiences while avoiding others. By purposefully considering which experiences might be empowering or limiting, you can make wiser choices over time.

This conscious awareness of which experiences you prefer will help you in your journey. Similarly, it is important to appreciate that regardless of the experience, you always have a choice in how you react to the circumstances. Even challenging experiences can be used for growth and future success depending on how you decide to process each life event.

Unlike material or tangible items, experiences are fleeting. They come and go. But over the course of your life, these experiences will provide a script of your life and your journey.

Those who want to realize their full potential in life can better attain these objectives by not only including specific experiences in their lives but by self-reflecting on them as well. These activities will help you progressively add value to your life.

> *It would be easy to fill this particular Pillar chapter with tales of those who have climbed Mount Everest or sailed around the world—you know, the traditionally "bold" experiences that make us all go "wow!" But there's an underlying theme to this book that has shaped and guided the words on every page, a theme of boldness as a form of giving back. And sure, while mountain climbing and sailing as experiences can enrich the self and inspire others, there's still a certain kind of altruism those impressive feats lack.*

> *True self-improvement leads to a better understanding of the world around us, and it puts*

us on a path to help make the world a better place.

Also, the funny thing about true self-improvement is that it doesn't require expensive equipment or training, or a sailboat, or anything like that. In fact, often, it requires that absence of those things.

Yes, I'm talking about the minimalist experience as a means of making yourself a better person and improving the world. And who better to use as an example than the man who made minimalism a key component of living a Bold Life?

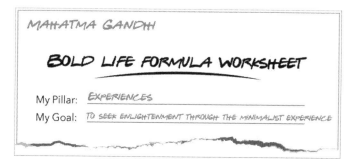

MAHATMA GANDHI

BOLD LIFE FORMULA WORKSHEET

My Pillar: EXPERIENCES
My Goal: TO SEEK ENLIGHTENMENT THROUGH THE MINIMALIST EXPERIENCE

Mahatma Gandhi was many things in his lifetime, including a lawyer, volunteer during the Boer War, father and husband, but his enduring image is that of a simply-clothed man whose austerity was a prevailing tenet (right up there with the whole non-violence and "freedom for India" thing, of course).

He didn't start out a minimalist. But somewhere along the timeline between him being tossed off a train in South Africa for not being white, and leading mass protests against British rule in India, Gandhi began eschewing the "excesses" of life—like Western-style clothes and foods more complex than naan bread and vegetables—and took to living as simple as possible.

That sheer simplicity of being became his modus operandi and the main principle of his core beliefs that resonated with millions.

Want an experience that will provide a level of understanding and enlightenment that few other experiences can provide?

Want an experience that will change the way one thinks and views the world?

Do what Gandhi did and live a minimalist lifestyle. It doesn't have to be anything extreme—you can be a minimalist for a week and gain insight and perspective from it.

As experiences go, it is by far the most inexpensive, most enlightening, and one most likely to put you on the path to giving back!

EXPERIENCES

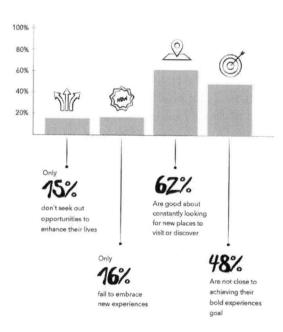

Only 15%
don't seek out opportunities to enhance their lives

62%
Are good about constantly looking for new places to visit or discover

Only 16%
fail to embrace new experiences

48%
Are not close to achieving their bold experiences goal

Research based on Project Bold Life Assessment at BoldLifeScore.com

SECTION III: ARE YOU READY TO LIVE A BOLD LIFE?

Chapter 18 – The Bold Life Assessment: Crunching the Numbers

The Bold Life Assessment was a significant effort. As a result, its impact on the book is significant. The accumulated data ultimately increased my passion for understanding how and why the book, the Bold Life Formula and worksheets could be helpful to anyone pursuing goals.

But first, some background.

The Bold Life Score is a customized proprietary web program that was built for research purposes for this book. Kudos goes to my team for doing such a great job. I have also thanked them in the acknowledgments.

It took months of effort to get a program that had the questions and content we wanted. The design of the product began in 2018. It also took time to design an interface that was fun and easy to use. We wanted to make it easy for people to answer the 48 questions and seven free-form fields. The final product was a good one.

Finally, the assessment was released publicly. We collected results from June 2019 until Feb 20, 2020, for purposes of statistics shared in the book. The assessment can be found at www.boldlifescore.com.

Here is a screenshot from the assessment landing page:

ASSESSMENT

Are You Living

A Bold Life?

Find out in less than 10 minutes!

Enter a valid email address

GET STARTED >

Account already exist? Login

Terms of Use | Privacy Policy

Over the course of those nine months, almost 2,000 people participated in the assessment, while almost 900 completed it. Clearly, they wanted to see the report and understand how they were doing!

The Bold Life Score Report (BLSR) is what participants receive upon completion. It is customized for everyone based on their unique answers. The programming for the grades and feedback was an extensive effort.

Here is an example of the BLSR:

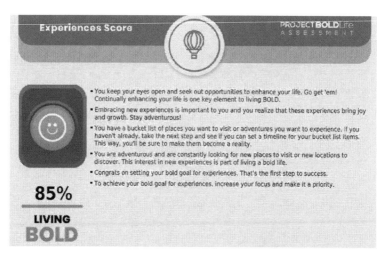

- You keep your eyes open and seek out opportunities to enhance your life. Go get 'em! Continually enhancing your life is one key element to living BOLD.
- Embracing new experiences is important to you and you realize that these experiences bring joy and growth. Stay adventurous!
- You have a bucket list of places you want to visit or adventures you want to experience. If you haven't already, take the next step and see if you can set a timeline for your bucket list items. This way, you'll be sure to make them become a reality.
- You are adventurous and are constantly looking for new places to visit or new locations to discover. This interest in new experiences is part of living a bold life.
- Congrats on setting your bold goal for experiences. That's the first step to success.
- To achieve your bold goal for experiences, increase your focus and make it a priority.

85%

LIVING
BOLD

The questions were designed to gain insight from people prior to book publication about their self-determined assessment of their goals, as well as progress towards them and general rankings of the Pillars. By design, we did not provide any guidance or assistance to anyone filling out the questionnaire.

Most People Stated They Have Bold Goals

Interestingly, 3.67 Bold Goals per person was the average. The distribution of goals was heavily centered between three to five goals.

Most People Believe They Are Not Making Good Progress

Across all goals, 67% assessed themselves as less than good. People generally are not doing well with Bold Goals.

A Shockingly High Percentage of People Need Help with Goal setting

A whopping 84% of respondents did not write a goal that was specific. In other words, they could not write a goal.

Those who free-formed their goal in the assessment wrote goals that simply did not qualify as a goal. Literally, hundreds and hundreds of non-goals were shared.

Here are some examples of "non-goals":

- Travel more
- Be conscious of my leadership
- Keep active and have fun
- Raise my children
- Travel
- Self-care
- Money
- Keep being a great stay-at-home mom and wife
- Make more, spend less
- Have good friends
- Visit family more
- Be secure

The problem with these ideas now that you have read this far in the book is easy for you to understand – 84% of respondent's goals were not specific enough or measurable in any way!

Very few were stretch. An amorphous goal is unachievable. For example, if your goal is to save money, would putting one penny in a piggy bank qualify?

As stated in previous chapters, many people confuse the concept of a Pillar or value with a goal. "Helping My Children" is not a goal. It is a value.

A goal would be much more specific. For example, a parenting goal could look like:

Pillar: Relationships, specifically parenting

Value: "I will help my child:

Goal: "I will save enough money by my daughter's 18th birthday (e.g., greater than $50,000.00) to help her pay for college and not incur large sums of debt. I will also provide education and development opportunities that will enable her to get accepted to a quality university at 18."

Understanding these distinctions is a critical part of success.

Balancing Bold Goals Was a Clear Issue for People

Some people had seven Bold Goals and stated they wanted to do it all. While this desire to achieve is to be applauded, the science shows most people can only handle two goals at a time.

Planning the Pillars and goals was clearly absent. Understanding goal timelines from the Pillar Planner Worksheet would have enabled people to specify the "when" of their Bold Goals more clearly.

Young People are Passionate About Bold Goals and Thinking About Bold Life Issues

About 50% of the participants were 25-years old or younger, while the remaining four older age bands were evenly distributed over the other 50% of participants.

The interest in Bold Goals by younger people seems obvious yet made me think about how to get messages across to younger participants. Hence, Boldy was born! If you just flip through the book and look at the images of Boldy and friends, you will get a strong idea of the key takeaways.

Visual learning is important, and I spent significant time "writing" the Project Bold Life story through Boldy. I hope you found him entertaining and inspiring.

The Assessment Results Led to More Effort in the Worksheets

As a result of assessment answers, it became clear that the specifics of the Formula needed to be built up with enough detail to enable people to not only increase their likelihood of success but to clearly understand the subtle differences.

The Pillars (the first part of the formula) are part of building a plan around your values and when you will spend efforts on them. The worksheets in goal setting help you to get to a specific, clear goal that enables you to then build a plan for accomplishment.

The worksheets on Action Plans clearly help bring together the important ingredients needed to foster success.

All of the participants' time is appreciated. If you took the Assessment, you helped make the entire book better and more insightful. Thank you!

Chapter 19 – Believe and Achieve

By now, you should have a firm grasp of the notion of bold living, and have burning inside you the desire to attain the Bold Life you want.

You should believe in yourself and in your ability to achieve whatever Bold Goals you set.

You now understand how to take on challenges and whether you should get back on the horse or embrace the blank sheet of paper.

You have the tools needed to succeed.

I hope you go down "Bold Road." And if you choose to go down that path, please take the time to complete each of the Worksheets.

They will help you determine where your interest lies within the context of the Seven Pillars, and refine those interests into Bold Goals.

They will keep you from getting lost in the indecision of Seesaw Park.

They will also help you put together the building blocks of your Action Plan, as well as prepare you for those times when you may fall off your horse.

And last but certainly not least, they will enable you to determine who can help you get back on track.

The Worksheets are distillations of the successes of others—like Vivica Fox and her commitment to both her mother and God, or the McCurry's action plan to reduce expenses and save their money, or Scott Young's refinement of his goals until he hit upon the one that would give him a life bolder than the one he'd originally imagined.

The Worksheets are important pieces of the puzzle. So, too, are all the stories that fueled them, for they should serve as your inspiration.

Maybe you don't have designs on someday becoming a superstar pro wrestler like Titus O'Neil, and it's possible you don't hope to reshape Church doctrine like Father Sirico.

But if you do, or if you simply want to walk again, retire at 33, or be the best spouse you can possibly be, PROJECT BOLD LIFE has hopefully shown you that it's possible and that the means to succeed are within your grasp.

Beyond all that, there's Boldy. Even if you barely skimmed the text, Boldy has been there all along, on his own journey to realizing a Bold Life. I'd like to think that his narrative thread has kept you engaged and flipping the pages.

This is the final chapter of the book, and with this chapter being written, I actually close a chapter as well – a Bold Goal achieved that hopefully inspires others for success. And it all started with a young man named Max who saw the challenges standing in between him and a better life, overcame them, and created a Bold Life for himself in America. Max Kopko was my grandfather.

His sacrifices, commitment to his plan, and his ability to deal with life-threatening challenges—from when he ventured out of Poland to when he started a family in the New World—became the foundation for all that I've accomplished—including writing PROJECT BOLD LIFE!

I know you can succeed with the tools and lessons laid out before you. And I want to hear those success stories, no matter how big or small your Bold Goal.

(You can contact me through my author site, EdKopko.com.)

APPENDIX 1: THE WORKSHEETS

INTRODUCTION

Welcome the the PROJECT BOLD LIFE worksheet booklets! These worksheets will serve as the tools needed to help you pick which of the Seven Pillars are most relevant to your Bold Goals. In addition, they will enable you to determine which goals should be tackled first, as well refine those goals so they are attainable. By the end, you should have an Action Plan laid out, and have a firm idea of what to do if you're ever derailed from pursuing your Bold Goal.

Good luck, and congrats on taking the first step towards a Bold Life!

PBL = PI + S²G + AP

$$PBL = (Pi) + S^2G + Ap$$

There are seven key areas that serve as sources of inspiration in defining what a Bold Life means to each of us. These areas-or pillars-are: **HEALTH, ACHIEVEMENT, CAREER, FINANCES, RELATIONSHIPS, GIVING BACK** and **EXPERIENCES**. Through the Seven Pillars, you can identify specific aspects of your life where you would like to set Bold Goals and live more boldy.

Which Pillars align with your **Bold Goals**? Which should you tackle first? The following worksheets will help you figure that out!

PILLAR RANKER

	IMPORTANCE	TIMING	WHY
HEALTH	○ Very Important ○ Important ○ Not Important	○ Now ○ Later ○ Much Later	_____
FINANCES	○ Very Important ○ Important ○ Not Important	○ Now ○ Later ○ Much Later	_____
CAREER	○ Very Important ○ Important ○ Not Important	○ Now ○ Later ○ Much Later	_____
ACHIEVEMENTS	○ Very Important ○ Important ○ Not Important	○ Now ○ Later ○ Much Later	_____
RELATIONSHIPS	○ Very Important ○ Important ○ Not Important	○ Now ○ Later ○ Much Later	_____
GIVING BACK	○ Very Important ○ Important ○ Not Important	○ Now ○ Later ○ Much Later	_____
EXPERIENCES	○ Very Important ○ Important ○ Not Important	○ Now ○ Later ○ Much Later	_____

- HEALTH — Both physical and mental well-being
- FINANCES — The fiscal wherewithal to survive and thrive
- CAREER — Work that fulfills
- ACHIEVEMENTS — Accomplishments you are proud of
- RELATIONSHIPS — Family, friends and everything in between
- GIVING BACK — Charity and volunteering;
- EXPERIENCES — Those memorable things that make life worth living

IMPORTANCE
VI - Very Important   I - Important

TIMING
Now   Later   Much Later

$PBL = H + S^2G + A$

PILLAR PLANNER

► What Pillars deserve attention now and what Pillars deserve attention later? By filling out which Pillars merited a "Very Important" ranking (from the Pillar Ranker worksheet) and accounting for which ones warrant immediate attention, this worksheet will help you visualize a long term plan.

	TODAY	5 YEARS	10 YEARS	20 YEARS	30 YEARS
HEALTH	○	○	○	○	○
ACHIEVEMENT	○	○	○	○	○
CAREER	○	○	○	○	○
FINANCE	○	○	○	○	○
RELATIONSHIP	○	○	○	○	○
GIVING BACK	○	○	○	○	○
EXPERIENCES	○	○	○	○	○

PBL = (1) + 5/G + Ay

$$PBL = Pi + \boxed{S^2G} + Ap$$

A crucial aspect of achieving any **Bold Life** is making **Bold Goals** and accomplishing them. But what exactly are **Bold Goals**? They are **SMART**, stretch goals that test your limits. These may be relative goals that compare you to others, or they may be "personal best" goals that invite value and deep meaning to your life. Either way, **Bold Goals** are special, and deserve some in-depth analysis and refinement. The following worksheets will help!

KNOW YOUR WHY
GOAL REFINER

▶ Every goal needs to be distilled down to its most basic motivation, for only in those "why" questions can true inspiration be found.

Start by putting your goal in the top box. Then move down to the box below it and answer the question "Why?" Then do it again, then again. Since the aim is to gain a better understanding of your motivations, your "Ultimate Why" will be the most distilled understanding of your goal.

▼ What is your goal?

▼ But why is that important?

▼ But why is that important?

▼ Why is this important to you?

▼ The Ultimate Why

PBL = PI + S/G + AP

PROJECT
BOLD
LIFE

BOLD GOALS
PROS VS. CONS

▶The execution of any Bold Goal will have an upside and a downside, both as they affect you and affect the world around you. Use this Pro vs. Con sheet to determine the cost/benefit analysis of your potential Bold undertaking.

My Bold Goal is _____

Self Pros	Self Cons
1.	1.
2.	2.
3.	3.
4.	4.
5.	5.
External Pros	**External Cons**
1.	1.
2.	2.
3.	3.
4.	4.
5.	5.

$PBL = PI + SG + AP$

$$PBL = Pi + S2G + \boxed{Ap}$$

Any true effort to accomplish a goal requires a strong **Action Plan**. This plan will lay out both long-term, strategic objectives, and smaller goals that go into meeting those objectives.

The following worksheets will help you iron out that Action Plan, and also determine who will provide support if you "fall of your horse" en route to your Bold Goal.

BUILDING BLOCK PLAN
WORKSHEET

▶ There will be multiple steps taken to accomplish your Bold Goal. At the top of each column, write down each of those steps. Below those steps, write down the tasks that must be completed to move on to the next step. This is your Action Plan, broken down into broader brushstrokes (at the top of the columns) and more granular details within each column.

My Bold Goal is: _____

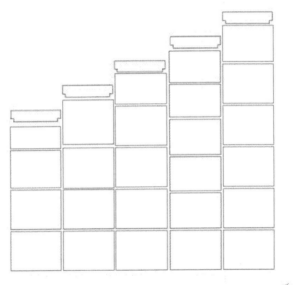

PBL = PI + SPG + AP

MY FALL OFF
THE HORSE PLANS

Type of Fall	Two ways to get back on

1. _____   ☐ _____
                                   ☐ _____

2. _____   ☐ _____
                                   ☐ _____

3. _____   ☐ _____
                                   ☐ _____

4. _____   ☐ _____
                                   ☐ _____

Sometimes a fall off the horse while galloping toward your Bold Goal is inevitable. How will you react? The best reaction is to be proactive · meaning, figure out what will likely make you fall, then determine how best to get back in the saddle.

$PBL = PI + S^2G + AP$

MY BOLD COMMITMENT
& SUPPORT TEAM

People I have made my Commitment public to (at least 2)   Date Completed

☐ _____   _____

☐ _____   _____

☐ _____   _____

People who will help me when I Fall Off the Horse   Date Asked

☐ _____   _____

☐ _____   _____

☐ _____   _____

PBL = Fi + SnG + Ap

MY BOLD GOALS
YEARLY PLAN

▶ What tasks do you need to accomplish on a yearly basis to reach your Bold Goals? What tasks do you need to accomplish yearly that have nothing to do with your Bold Goals? Use this worksheet to layout both kinds of tasks. Once that's done, you will get a better sense of the things on that might be distracting you. You will at least get a better handle on things that are keeping you from your goal!

Yearly Tasks for Accomplishing Bold Goal

1. _____
2. _____
3. _____
4. _____
5. _____

Yearly Tasks Unrelated to Accomplishing Bold Goal

1. _____
2. _____
3. _____
4. _____
5. _____

PBL = PI + S²G + AP

MY BOLD GOALS
MONTHLY PLAN

▶ What tasks do you need to accomplish on a monthly basis to reach your Bold Goals? What tasks do you need to accomplish monthly that have nothing to do with your Bold Goals? Use this worksheet to layout both kinds of tasks. Once that's done, you will get a better sense of the things on that might be distracting you. You will at least get a better handle on things that are keeping you from your goal!

Monthly Tasks for Accomplishing Bold Goal

1. _____
2. _____
3. _____
4. _____
5. _____

Monthly Tasks Unrelated to Accomplishing Bold Goal

1. _____
2. _____
3. _____
4. _____
5. _____

$PBL = Pi + S^2G + AP$

MY BOLD GOALS
DAILY PLAN

► What tasks do you need to accomplish on a daily basis to reach your Bold Goals? What tasks do you need to accomplish daily that have nothing to do with your Bold Goals? Use this worksheet to layout both kinds of tasks. Once that's done, you will get a better sense of the things on that might be distracting you. You will at least get a better handle on things that are keeping you from your goal!

Daily Tasks for Accomplishing Bold Goal

1. _____
2. _____
3. _____
4. _____
5. _____

Daily Tasks Unrelated to Accomplishing Bold Goal

1. _____
2. _____
3. _____
4. _____
5. _____

$PBL = PI + S^2G + Ap$

BOLD LIFE FORMULA WORKSHEET

▶ Who will help you if you fall off the horse en route to your Bold Goal? Who is part of your Bold Support Team? Give a signed Bold Life Formula Worksheet to at least two members of your Support Team, and list who they are and when you gave them the sheets. Below that, list anyone else who might help you - via encouragement, motivation, or whatever.

My Goal: ....

My Pillar: ....

Is it Smart?   Yes ☐   No ☐

Is it Stretch?   Yes ☐   No ☐

Why is this Pillar inspirational to me?

....

....

Do I have my Fall Off The Horse Plan?   Yes ☐   No ☐

Do I have my Support Team?   Yes ☐   No ☐

My Action Plan

GOAL

STEP 5

STEP 4

STEP 3

STEP 2

STEP 1

I hereby affirm that my Action Plan is laid out,
my commitment is made public, and I have a Support Team

$BL = P_i + S^2G + A_p$

APPENDIX II: INDEX

3

33 Reasons to Live Bold · 6

A

Action Plan · 112, 114, 141
Acton Institute · 102, 210, 212

B

Bold Cartoon
  Bold accomplishment versus not-so-bold accomplishment · 44
  Boldy and Ed · 229
  Boldy and the Little Engine That Tried · 156
  Boldy at Bold Mountain · 4
  Boldy at the top of Bold Mountain · 231
  Boldy having tea with the Queen and Queen · 14
  Boldy prepared for his climb · 148
  Boldy with his family · 190
  Building Blocks to Bold Goals · 116
  Don't Get Lost in Seesaw Park · 114
  Falling off the horse · 40
  Geddy Lee of Rush · 49
  Max · 230

Bold Commitment and Support Team · 121
Bold Goals · 3, 56, 59, 66, 74, 82, 83, 88, 143
Bold Life · 51, 83
  defined · 13
Bold Life Formula · 45, 46, 108, 109, 133
Bold Story
  Amy Chua · 198
  Dr. Laraine Lloyd · 10, 161
  Father Sirico · 10, 47, 101, 209
  Henry Stifel · 10, 31, 206
  Justin and Kaisorn McCurry · 9, 51, 134
  Mahatma Gandhi · 218
  Marilyn Reyes Scales · 9, 191
  Max · 77, 94, 109, 167, 230
  Pam Sloate · 9, 33, 151
  RJ Garbowicz · 9, 177
  Scott Young · 9, 18, 170
  Titus O'Neil · 9, 47, 175
  Vinod · 10, 185
  Vivica Fox · 47, 123
Building Block Plan · 116

C

Call of the Entrepreneur · 102
Charles Koch Institute · 192, 194
Christopher and Dana Reeve Foundation · 206
Christopher Reeve Foundation · 207
Clarkson, Kelly · 26

D

Daily Implementation Plan
· 131
Diversity MBA Magazine ·
123
Dystonia Muse · 152

E

Ellis Island · 95, 109, 110

F

Fall Off the Horse Plan ·
119
Fitzgerald, Sister Tesa ·
192
Frankl, Viktor · 27

G

Gilder, George · 102
Growth of MOOCs · 20

H

Hone, Dr. Lucy · 23, 26, 27

I

Impact Prisons 2017: The
Future of the
Correctional System ·
192
ImpactNYC · 192
Incarceration Rates
Worldwide · 195

M

Mauren, Kris · 102
McElvane, Pam · 123
Monthly Implementation
Plan · 131

N

Norcross, John · 99, 104,
136, 171

P

PBL Assessment
Research · 9, 223, 224
Achievement · 168
Career · 183
Experiences · 220
Finances · 189
Giving Back · 215
Health · 158
Relationships · 203

R

Reddy, Vikrant · 192, 194
Root of Good Earnings &
Wealth graph · 54

S

Scott, Randy · 28
Seesaw Park · 113
Seven Pillars · 15, 56, 59
SMART · 83, 87
Steiner, Edward A. · 95,
109
Stretch and Inspirational ·
90

Synapse Innovation
    Conference · 175

T

Tierney, Maura · 72
Types of Challenges · 25
Types of Positive
    Challenges · 26

V

Vance, Cyrus Jr. · 192

W

Wilderotter, Peter · 207
Worksheet
    Bold Goals - Pros vs.
        Cons, example · 136
    Bold Goals, Pros vs.
        Cons · 89
    Bold Life Formula · 133
    Building Block Plan ·
        118

Building Block Plan,
    example · 135, 196
Goal Refiner · 63
Goal Refiner, example ·
    174
My Bold Commitment &
    Support Team · 122
My Bold Commitment &
    Support Team,
    example · 166
My Bold Goals - Monthly
    Plan · 132
My Bold Goals - Yearly
    Plan · 130
My Fall Off the Horse
    Plans · 120
Pillar Planner · 67
Pillar Planner, example ·
    69
Pillar Ranker · 50
Pillar Ranker, example ·
    80, 214

Y

Yearly Implementation
    Plan · 131

About the Author

Bold Business CEO and publisher Ed Kopko, previously the CEO of Butler International and Chief Executive Magazine, racked up an extensive list of media appearances and publishing credits over the years--from *CNBC* to *Forbes*, the *Wall Street Journal*, and other outlets. Ed has seen success take many forms for many different people – from entrepreneurs to celebrities to people just trying to improve themselves and the world at large. The PROJECT BOLD LIFE book was born from his observations and interactions with countless people who overcame hardship and achieved success.

Ed's work in the diversity and inclusion movement garnered him the prestigious 2019 Impact Award from Diversity MBA Magazine.

He splits his time between New York City and St. Petersburg, FL, and finds time to meditate daily.

Made in the USA
Columbia, SC
22 August 2020